Pastor Sir
+
AnneMarie   I hope this one
inspires and encourages
you. Matthew 19:26
Buy Bul

We can do all things through HE who
strengthens us.
            God Bless, Adam Elbb

I hope this book touches you
and whoever you might
share its stories with in
a special and divine way.
            Clay

Cover photos:

Top left corner of cross, clockwise from left: Josh Swickard, Justin Paul, Cody Anthony, Dani Santana, Derek Brown, Jordi & Kaitlin Vilasuso

Top right of cross, clockwise from left: Gary Casaletto, Adam Ellenberger, Tim & Colleen Lucas, Justin Kendrick, Cuyler Black and Nate & Amanda Goyco.

Bottom left of cross, clockwise from left: Rick Mostacero, Tawana "Tee" Fields, Dave Brooks, Josh Santibañez, Victor Cardona and Kyle & Michell Ellsworth.

Bottom right of cross, clockwise from left: Kayra Montañez, Clay Thompson, Sydney & CeeJay Larino, James Apap, JP Robinson and Alex Soares.

Our Walk With Him

Bryan Beckley

With:
Cody Anthony
James Apap
Cuyler Black
Dave Brooks
Derek Brown
Victor Cardona
Gary Casaletto
Adam Ellenberger
Kyle and Michell Ellsworth
Tawana "Tee" Fields
Nate and Amanda Goyco
Justin Paul Kahn
Justin Kendrick
CeeJay and Sydney Larino
Tim and Colleen Lucas
Kayra Montañez
Rick Mostacero
JP Robinson
Josh Santibanez
Dani Santana
Alex Soares
Josh Swickard
Clay Thompson
Jordi and Kaitlin Vilasuso

Our Walk With Him

Library of Congress Cataloging-In-Publication Data is available

ISBN # 9798849588681

This book is dedicated to my brother Mark Beckley, who went home to be with God while this book was being written. You are missed every single day.

To those of you reading this book that feel like you are far away from God, trust me, He is right there beside you.

Contents:

Introduction

"Bryan, you are more than just a gay man." Close your eyes, picture the kindest, most loving and genuinely good person you know and say those words to yourself, "you're more than just", ending it with how you identify yourself. Whether it is mom, dad, gay, straight, construction worker, doctor, homeless, ill. Erase all of those things that identify you and lean into the only identity that matters, which is that you are His child. Abby Taylor said those nine words to me, and it was the beginning of the strongest part of my walk with God that I have known and am still currently on. That walk will only be altered when my time here on Earth is done and I am living in eternity with God. The words that follow and the stories of the people in this book are meant to bring hope to your life and inspire you. If there is anything I have learned throughout the entirety of my life, it is that words matter. This book was put out with love and the desire to bring you closer to Him.

This was taken at my baptism on Christmas Eve, 2020. That night changed the entire direction of my life. Pictured, from left: Michell Ellsworth, Clint Taylor, Abby Taylor, Tawana "Tee" Fields, Rich Lem, Kyle Ellsworth and Cuyler Black

My Walk With Him

As the finishing touches were being put on my first book, *A Time To Heal: Stories of Hope & Inspiration*, I started going through this enormous change in my life. Those of you who have read that book will certainly recall that. The world was finally starting to open back up after six months of lockdowns. There was a sense that life would return to some sense of normalcy. The churches we so desperately missed being a part of for in-person worship and praise were finally reopening their doors.

Liquid Church's Morris County campus in Parsippany, NJ, was reopening in September 2020 for outdoor services, and I was all in. I missed serving and could not wait to jump back into doing so. The week the church resumed in-person, outdoor services, I signed up to serve on Guest Connections. While all of Liquid's campuses were not opening at the time, the broadcast campus in Parsippany did.

I had started attending Liquid Church in September of 2019 at one of the locations that was closer to my house. We were just about to move into a bigger building to accommodate all of the people that God was bringing through our doors when *bam*, the world shut down because of Covid.

What followed was a season of online church services each week. They were still structured in the same way, with worship sets that were part of a normal Sunday, followed by a message from our lead pastor, Tim Lucas.

It was great to be able to at least feel like we were all part of the community even though we could not be in person, hugging, holding hands, praying and lifting each other up. As the summer went on, I started losing the steam I had gathered while serving in person. I think many of us who were serving were by then. It was easy to get frustrated being locked in our homes with limited contact with anyone we did not live with.

The sermons started to not hit in the same way. Church began to feel like a scheduled, one-hour "chore" that I was so used to doing while I was growing up in the Catholic faith. During that time of being shut in, worship music became the thing that would always keep me strongly connected to Him. Music in general has gotten me through every hardship I have faced, but worship music was feeding me differently than music in the past. Each week, new worship sets with a limited worship team and new sermons were recorded from our broadcast campus to be run on Sundays and throughout the week. I started to feel alive again. Even though it was not a return to normal, it was a step in the right direction.

Working in front of a computer all day from home, only to be followed by more screen-time doing Zoom meetings or watching television, the only entertainment you could get at the time, was leading to burnout and fatigue. Don't get me wrong. I loved and was grateful to still be working, but even that is not the same when you are just stuck at your computer without interaction with your co-workers in person. The silver lining was that after commuting to the city for the better part of 15 years, off and on, I did not have to worry about train schedules, rude commuters, heat, cold, lugging bags, traffic and all of the other issues that go with commuting on public transit.

Something started to change though, and it is something I say to myself, even when I feel low and cannot find joy, is "but God".

I have been through many, many serious challenges in my life that started from a very young age. Physical abuse and sexual abuse, intense bullying and the loss of my father all occurred before I was out of my early 20s. There were many, many times when I felt lost and alone. I was not strong in my faith like1 I am now. All of my *"Why Gods"* became *"But Gods"* though, when I started serving again at church in the fall of 2020.

I had been a member of the Guest Connections team when the church shut down. Guest connections is exactly what it sounds like. You welcome the new guests, make them feel connected to the church and answer any questions they have. It was a very people-oriented serving opportunity, which is right in my wheelhouse. I am very social and outgoing by nature. When the church reopened, I started serving again on that team. Liquid Church's broadcast campus in Parsippany, NJ is huge, and we opened to what became like a drive-in movie atmosphere. People parked and either sat in their cars, or in chairs in front of their cars. Everyone had been cooped up for so long, that it seemed like Christmas morning just to be able to do that.

As a member of guest connections, we would walk up and down the aisles of the massive parking lot and greet each guest, welcome them and talk as much as we could. We were met with the same happiness that we were feeling by serving. Everyone was happy to be back in person, even if it was not the same as when the building was open. There was live worship again, live messages from our pastors and also a sense of community.

In those first few weeks, I was meeting so many new people. The campus locations had less guests and staff when we first reopened, so you become tightknit very quickly. The broadcast campus seemed overwhelming, by the sheer volume of guests, staff and volunteers, even though it was still the thick of the pandemic, relative to a smaller campus. But it was there at Liquid's broadcast campus where I would meet people who have changed my life in more ways than I could articulate. I have gained mentors, many who appear on these pages, friends, and brothers and sisters in Christ. I became part of the community and assimilated very quickly by stepping in to serve anywhere I could.

Before the pandemic shut everything down, the pastor would run through his message on Thursday, which was recorded for church online. When we reopened, because we were restricted in capacity, those Thursday recordings became a full-on experience, with the worship set also recorded to go along with the message for those not coming back in person. Due to the other campuses not reopening, some of the members from where I was attending branched off to a different location, while some came up to the broadcast campus. Our team hosted the Thursday night recordings, which were called TNL. It was great to be able to add a second day of worship and word. It gave me the opportunity to make more connections with people.

As I met more and more people from the broadcast campus, I started making new friends. I joined a small group led by three guys, who would become the captains steering my ship through the waters of change that was starting to occur. Kyle Ellsworth (who is featured in the book), David Ramirez and Rich Lem, became the closest guy friends I had had in my life. Although small group was still virtual, it at least led to feeling more like a part of the church community, plus we would see each other either on Thursday or Sundays, as well as Wednesday for group. I was starting to build community with other Christians that put their faith ahead of anything else.

I was finding my wings as a Christian and through small group, I was part of a community of guys that deeply cared for each other and provided a safe space to share anything and everything going on in our lives. Small groups are safe places where things said there stay there.

As the fall progressed, outreaches began to occur. The first large event I served at was for the Christmas outreach in December of 2020. Liquid hosted a huge outdoor, Winter Wonderland event with everything from reindeer stands that had games and prizes, a living nativity, different photo experiences and more. That concluded with the children of families who could not afford toys meeting Santa and being given a toy that the parents chose at the start of the event.

My men's small group was part of the living nativity. That was the first serving opportunity that I was part of that really started to strengthen that bond with the guys. Some of the connections had already been cemented and some needed a little more watering to get where they are today. It was an intense time for me, because I was still trying to reconcile my sexuality and my faith. While I had accepted God into my life, I also let my entire identity be defined by my sexuality and outgoing personality. There were tough adjustments to be made because there was still church hurt in my heart from the way I had been treated in the past. But I decided to trust God and what He was doing in my life at the time. It was not always comfortable, but being a Christian is not supposed to be. There were times I felt uncomfortable and defensive.

During one small group we started going through the book of Romans. For a Christian whose only interactions with church were negative based on their sexual identity, this led me to feeling attacked. As we sat online and read through the chapter, I felt I was "less than", not deserving of God's love and that the entire discussion was going to be pointed at me. I put a wall up, got very defensive with Rich and ended up making up a lie about my boss calling, so I could get off the meeting.

I was so hurt, so angry and felt rejected. I had finally felt like I had been assimilating and was not being judged, yet here was a book that is harsh in terms of homosexuality. All of the Catholic guilt that was imparted on me, "you're going to hell," "you're evil," "you're a pedophile who is mentally ill," came rushing back to the surface and I sure as heck was not going to be made to feel that way by the guys who I trusted to help guide me on my walk. The trouble is, that was not what Rich was doing. I took it as a personal attack, like I always had. I did not understand being part of a church community where you were not judged by your sin. Sin is sin. It took me a long time to reconcile myself with that fact. But that outburst did not stop the guys from pouring into me. I signed back on that night after David checked on me via text and I apologized for storming off the Zoom. Kyle would later tell me that he brought it up prior to the meeting that I might react negatively. It takes a lot of time to get over the hurt inflicted by a church and clearly, I was not over it.

As the weeks went on, my bond with the guys continued to grow. We would pray for each other, check in on each other and were always a call away. They held me up in times I could not do it myself and were rocks as I was developing and strengthening my relationship with God, and the three of them are still doing it today. Kyle became my best friend, who many times has dropped everything to come and help me, stand by my side, be my sounding board and encourage me. Through him I started serving more. David is a strong brother to me. It is always so hard to describe him and his role in my life. The easy copout is… "It's just David…he is a mensch. How could you not love him?" But he is a young man who has gone through his own challenges and always inspires me to see things in a different light. He is easygoing, fun to be around and a true friend. Rich is the one who challenges me the most, and I mean that in a good way. Rich answers your question with a question and does not give you an easy out. He has taken me under his wing to study the Bible and I now lead my own men's group.

From the end of September 2020 until December of 2020 my life turned into "all God, all the time". It felt good to be the closest I had ever been to Him in my whole life. He had seen me through so many things up to that point, but this was the beginning of something that felt different inside. I started praying more, reading more devotionals, serving Him and surrounding myself with people from the church.

I had been baptized as a baby in the Catholic church, but as the months went by on my newly fresh walk with God, I made the decision that I wanted to be baptized at Liquid and I wanted it to be done before the end of the year. At Liquid they do baptisms two Sundays a year, but they had not yet started doing those again, because it is done in two big tubs in front of a full house.

I was not even sure that I would be able to handle something like that, given the nature of some of the sexual abuse that occurred in my past. I have a very hard time with being forced down, whether in water or not. It triggers me and I raised that concern. I also wanted to be baptized before the end of the year to cement the commitment I was making to Him. Between Thanksgiving and Christmas, church is full of outreaches, services, preparations for the holiday and then culminating with four services on Christmas Eve. The pastor in charge of the baptisms, Cuyler, who is also featured in the book, knew that it was something that I wanted to do before the end of the year, but things were just not lining up. I also wanted specific people to be there who were important on my walk up until that point within Liquid.

I served at the first service and left for the second and third service, then came back to serve at the fourth. That morning, Pastor Cuyler said that there was a chance they would be able to do it after the fourth service and that almost everyone that I wanted there was serving in some capacity that day. He said he would let me know later in the day if the baptism was actually going to be able to happen. I was on my way home and he called to tell me he would be able to do the baptism and that he would try his best to get everyone I requested to stay.

Now this was on Christmas Eve, the people had all served four services by the end of the day. They had all arrived by 6:30 a.m. and the last service was not going to be over until after 7. It had already started raining and was turning into snow. Everyone involved had places to go, whether it was to have dinner with family or travel to other states for the holiday. Each person that was asked, said yes to staying to watch me take this very important step on my walk with Him and I will be forever grateful to them. Kyle was there with (his wife now) Michell, Rich was there, Abby Taylor (who started this journey for me with that sentence that opened the book) and Tee (who you will meet in the book also), were by my side as Pastor Cuyler and Abby's husband, Pastor Clint, baptized me with water from the Jordan River.

Imagine being baptized on the night of Jesus's birth with water from the river He was baptized in, surrounded by the people who God has put in your life that have been building you up. It was overwhelming, to say the least. When you are baptized you are supposed to give a few words, but I could barely get out two words before tears started to flow. I could not believe the enormity of what was happening to me. I remember Cuyler and Clint blessing me with the water, the prayers they said over me and this feeling of peace, calm, tranquility and quite honestly. being reborn. I felt like every hurt, every anger, every sadness, everything, was washed away. It was honestly a supernatural feeling that I had never experienced before in my life. That night, surrounded by those people and in the hands of God, I became a new person.

Pastor Clint and Pastor Cuyler baptizing me

As the new year began, I continued serving on Guest Connections and also joined the social media team to help Tee get content for Instagram and Facebook. Being led by her on the team was incredible. I cannot say enough good things about Tee. She is a mentor, a friend, a class act and a teacher. I learned so much from her and not just by serving under her. We would talk for hours on the phone and she would help me navigate things. She is a rock, a constant and a gift from above. They don't call her Queen Tee for nothing. I had a great time serving under her because it combined the social aspects of interacting with the church members and staff of Liquid Church and because it was a responsibility I was entrusted with. You will learn just how special she is reading about her in the pages of the book and I know that she will inspire you.

I started getting the desire to serve on the media team as well. The musicians and tech people were who I would hang out with in high school while involved in theater class. They were like the gang of "misfits" who did not quite know what clique they "belonged" to, but all stuck together.

When you walk into Liquid Church's broadcast campus, you do not realize how many technical aspects there are to hosting services each week. Our campus holds 1,200 people. There is a stage where the worship set is performed and where the pastor speaks from. There is a control room that looks like the control room of a broadcast television studio. There are tons of lights, a sound board and a row of high-tech video cameras in the back of the room that capture each and every moment from different vantage points.

Some of you may be reading this thinking, "that isn't church to me" and I respect that. I also had that same thought the first time I went to the broadcast campus when I joined Liquid in September 2019. It didn't "feel" like church to me after being raised Catholic. When I stood, I always had my hands clasped together at my waist. Church is not about the building, it is not about the pastor, it is not about the worship team or traditions. Church is a hospital.

The heart of Liquid Church is the people. Growing up, I never felt connected while attending Saint Joseph's Roman Catholic church in my hometown. It was more of a chore to go each Sunday. My parents, my brother, sister and I went as a family each week. Unless you were sick or dead, you had to go. You also should be paying attention and not laughing or goofing off. While I never felt connected at church, it did connect my family and I. Faith was important to us.

While listening to the homily each week, I always felt like an outsider because of my same-sex attraction. It was always, "gays are going to hell, repent!" After a while you start to believe that and the place that is supposed to be bringing you closer to God is actually pushing you farther away from Him.

The straw that broke the camel's back for me was when my father died. He converted to Catholicism when he and my mom got married. He faithfully went to church every week. We had to have his funeral on a Saturday and the church also had a wedding planned that day at 1 p.m. When we made the arrangements, the priest at the time told my mom we could not have a full mass with communion, because of the time constraint. We were unhappy with that as were multiple other friends of ours who went to the church. No matter how much we pleaded, they would not budge. Let's face it, handing out communion at a funeral does not take that much time and even when you add in the prayers that go along with it, it would be 10 to 15 minutes max, and the funeral started at 9:30 or 10. The priest was not having it, even when others stepped in on our behalf. This is a church we went to for the better part of 20 years.

So, we reached out to the church my dad was going to for masses that were being said for cancer patients once a month, and the priest there was honored to give my father the proper service that he deserved. My dad died and was buried the week before Christmas, so it was a big day of extra collections for money. A number of our church friends put a letter in the offering envelope saying that their Christmas offering was going to the church that had buried my father. The priest (at our family church) then wrote in the bulletin to say that despite what people were hearing, none of it was true. I honestly was in shock. I never set foot in that church again. That was also the beginning of the end for me when it came to Catholicism.

I would go with my mom to the new church where my father had been going monthly for the special masses, but then it became the same, "you're going to hell, you are all sinners" repent, rinse and repeat. I then became a "holiday Catholic", which used to annoy me. Easter and Christmas, that was it. My mother is still Catholic today and my sister teaches at a Catholic school. Things have definitely changed, but the damage was done for me.

While it did shake my relationship with God a little, He never once left my side. That is who God is. Even in our ignorance, anger, rage and tears, He is there to comfort us. Sometimes you just need a person of the flesh to lead you back into your calling.

That person for me was DeVon Franklin. I loved the way DeVon delivered a message. My default is to say preached, but he is not a preacher. He was the one person who picked me up out of despair, dusted off my shoes and said, "keep walking". His words meant so much to me and resonated so deeply. Our friendship happened organically, and he is still a close mentor of mine today. He graciously took part in my first book and remains someone I can turn to when I need to hear an encouraging word. DeVon was the match strike that lit the flame of me finding a more modern church, with music that I related to, instead of hymns. He was the first person I called a mentor, but he would not be the last.

This is the perfect segue to talk about one of my closest mentors at Liquid Church, Clint Taylor. Clint is the Worship Experience Pastor and led worship on those weekly recordings during the pandemic. God granted Clint an undeniable talent with his singing ability. Not only is he amazing vocally and on electric guitar, you could really tell that he is not up on that platform to be "famous" or be seen.

I mentioned earlier that music had always gotten me through the toughest times in my life. There is something about a vocalist's ability to resonate with their audience. I was only listening to worship music from Liquid at the time and Brittany Iskander and Clint were the ones leading worship during the pandemic.

The first few times speaking to Clint were very awkward, for me at least. I decided to show my appreciation for how much I was impacted by he and the other members of the worship team by making face masks with their photos adorned across it, with crosses and Bible verses/sayings and the like. In my heart and my head, I knew that I was not idolizing any of them but showing my appreciation for the part of my life that they were enriching, this newfound desire to put God at the center of my life. That sounds like it makes sense and it certainly did in my head. Well, when you are new, and you show up to a place wearing face masks with people's likenesses on them, in hindsight it was a bit ...weird. Live and learn, right?

The thing that did not hit me until later was that although I thought God placed Clint in my life for his voice – vocally as the worship leader – it would become clear that Clint was placed on my walk to hear His voice.

Once the weirdness of the face masks dissipated a little, I felt more comfortable being myself. Occasionally I would ask Clint questions about things I was going through. He would give me advice and pray over me.

Flashback to the baptism: In the "old Bryan" brain, it was imperative that Clint and Abby be part of the baptism with Tee, Kyle, Rich, Cuyler and Michell. They were beyond gracious and stayed after serving at church for 13 hours and with a three-hour drive ahead of them in the rain and on the wet snowy roads en route to their Christmas celebrations with family. My baptism was the first time that I had a supernatural occurrence where Clint was involved.

The second supernatural occurrence came in June of 2021. By this time, I was pretty enmeshed with serving and was at Liquid Church's Morris County location with more frequency. It was a day that I will never forget and that quite literally scared me more than I cared to show that day. I had been taking prescription strength Naprosyn because I had hurt my back. I also tend to have an "all day buffet" eating habit (Compulsive Overeating Disorder), so I was snacking on almonds, cheese, strawberries and cherries. See, I can eat healthy! I started getting a tightness in my throat area and my voice started to change a little. I did not think much of it and went down to see Kyle, who was with his mid-week volunteers. They were celebrating a birthday and, you know, cake. When I came into the production room, my voice had changed even more, and I did not feel right. My face was also starting to swell. Kyle looked concerned, but there was time for concern, once I had cake. My voice was noticeably changing rapidly, and everyone started to notice. I had Benadryl at my desk, so I took that, but it did nothing.

It was also the day of an all-staff meeting, so all of the employees were there. Pastor Dave Brooks is married to a wonderful and loving woman named Lois, who just so happens to be an R.N. Once I realized that this situation was not getting any better, Kyle and I went to look in the auditorium for her, hoping there was an EpiPen in the building. Clearly, whatever was happening was not good. My eyes were almost swollen shut and I could not really speak. Thankfully I could still breathe. She insisted on calling an ambulance, which I did not want, because of my $3,000 out-of-pocket medical deductible. Well, she was having none of that and took over my care.

As we waited in the lobby for the ambulance, a police officer arrived and was trying to ask me questions. It got to the point where I could barely get out two words and my face was getting even more swollen. I could see the concern on Kyle and Lois's faces, and even though I was trying to stay calm, I could tell I looked as bad as I felt. Lois asked if wanted anything and I said, "Clint, prayer" and she asked me again because it was hard to understand. I repeated, "Clint, prayer."

Kyle stepped away to get Clint out of the staff meeting and he came out to pray over me. While I do not remember every word he said, I remember "I command the enemy out of Bryan" while he placed his hand directly on my back. I would love to tell you that a demon pushed me to the ground and scurried away and I went back to my day, but it was not like that. But something supernatural did start to occur. Water started dripping out of my lips like percolating coffee and also dripping from my face. By that point the ambulance arrived and when they loaded me up, I was full on drenched with water coming from everywhere; my mouth, nose, head. They did not even have enough gauze, towels or blankets to keep up with it. That freaked me out a bit, because I did not know what was happening.

Once I got to the E.R., they shot me up with two doses of epinephrine and also an IV of steroids. I ended up being in the hospital for three days. That was how serious a reaction I had. As I was lying in that ambulance, I managed to get out, "what happening?" and paramedic said it was my body's way of getting rid of the toxin.

I knew that it was much more than that. Some may think I am crazy, or may not be believers, but I am certain that God used Clint that day as a vessel to save me. So, baptism and anaphylaxis. Crazy coincidence that Clint was at both. That is all it must have been, right?

The weekend I came back to church happened to be Pride weekend. I was excited to get back to see everyone who was concerned for me, praying for me. After service Pastor Tim and his wife, Colleen, were in the lobby as they often are after each service. He came right up to me to ask how I was and they both prayed over me. When they finished praying over me, I started to explain a little about what had happened. I also asked if he knew what that weekend was and he said, "Pride, right?" I confirmed that he was correct and told him that I had spent the last two days after being discharged cleaning out all of the things that I associated with "gay pride" – the flags, the decorations, everything. In my heart, I knew that the one thing I was proud of was my walk with God. That is not to say everyone should throw away what makes them feel themselves or seen. It is also not permission for those in the gay community to throw stones at me. This is simply my journey.

About two months after that, I was serving on Guest Connections and the social media team, but I also wanted to try my hand on the production team. I was introduced to Rick Mostacero and started shadowing different roles. When you serve on the production team, you are needed for the entirety of the day, whereas I could do Guest Connections and social media together. This went on for a month where I would serve one Sunday on production then the next on the other two teams. If there was a place or an outreach to serve at, I was in, all day, every day and twice on Sunday. I was given the advice that I should choose one of the three teams I was serving on and focus 100 percent of my attention to that one team. No one questioned my giving 100 percent to whichever team I was serving on any given Sunday, but a focus on one team was ideal.

I decided that I really wanted to stay on the media team and although that was the least of the three teams where my social nature would be utilized, something in my heart told me to take that leap. It was God. What I did not realize at the time was that not only was He going to reinforce Clint's role on my walk, but He had also placed Rick in my life as a mentor. I had not known Rick very well at the time of my baptism, but he would later tell me that he was standing in the distance watching the ceremony.

The more that I served on the media team, the more I saw how Clint and Rick led. They encourage and lift their teams up. I swear the building could be burning down around Rick and he would not let on that he was concerned and would be calm. I was like, what is wrong with these two? Don't they know you have to lose it when things stress you out?

Through them, I have learned what it looks like to be a great leader, how to treat your team, how to encourage people, but also keep things real. One of the things that has really stuck with me, and this has been said multiple times by each of them, is that God has given us all unique giftings and we use those giftings to bring people closer to Him. None of us should be serving on a Sunday for our own gain or to showcase our talents for our own personal gain.

During Wednesday night rehearsals and right after Sunday morning tech rehearsals, they take turns leading the media and worship teams in prayer and reading a devotional or a quick Bible teaching. That always puts us in the proper posture for what is to come, and I look forward to it. I carry those words close to me.

At this point we are up to two supernatural occurrences that Clint was part of. There was a message series about identity and how we see ourselves. It was around this time that I was realizing the more I leaned into God, the more I surrounded myself with the people I was around, the less importance I put on my sexuality and identity as a gay man. Now, this could be the portion of the book where you start with the "brainwashing or gay conversion" thoughts.

But, none of that would be rooted in truth. This particular message really stuck a chord with me for some reason and as Pastor Tim spoke, I completely lost it. I mean, big crocodile tears that were dropping all over the place, which was affecting my ability to see what I was doing as the teleprompter operator. I kept trying to pull myself together, but in those moments the gratitude that I had for what God had done in my life and the people He put in it, I fully realized my true identity was as God's child. No other identity mattered. I had already taken steps in that direction, but this Sunday it hit.

As I tried to compose myself, I looked over to my left just to take my eyes off what I was doing for a second and lo and behold, Clint was standing there listening to the message. That brought an immediate sense of comfort to me and I was able to pull it together and finish out the service.

Afterward, I ran into him backstage, looked him dead in the eyes and with tears welling up again, I said, "You.... why is it *always* you?" He of course had no idea what I was talking about because he did not know I was upset during service. When I explained what happened, he said it is all God. I said, "I know, and I am not committing idolatry believing you are higher than Him. I just don't understand why it is always you." The whole "idolatry" nonsense is of my own doing because of those darn masks and how I thought I was perceived.

The most recent, but I am positive not the last, was the day of my brother's funeral. It had been a grueling week dealing with the sudden loss, on top of my mom and I doing everything in our power to keep our 14-year-old dog alive. As the mourners began paying their final respects, the emotions were overtaking my mom, sister and me. I was trying to be as strong as possible for them and I was just about to lose it, when I looked to my right and saw Clint and Abby in the line of mourners. Well, I did in fact lose it because it was just another example of God knowing who I needed to be there in that exact moment to bring me the strength to get through it. Clint had just lost his father a month prior, so it brought me an extra sense of peace knowing that someone who had just recently suffered an immediate close family member passing, was there at that exact moment I was about to say my final goodbye. As I looked to my left, his wife, Abby, was crouched down comforting my mom, whom she had never met before. That was the very embodiment of who I described in the first sentence of the book. The Taylors have played an enormous part on my walk with God and I am eternally grateful to and for them.

Clint has prayed over me many times, has been a constant support system in the heavy things, like the loss of my brother, and makes time for me when I need to talk something through. If you are excited to get to his chapter in the book, I need to manage your expectations – his words do not grace the pages. He politely and respectfully declined. Clint is so gracious that when I started writing the book, I messaged him and said that the book just did not feel complete without his presence in it in the form of an interview. He received that and encouraged me to be excited about this journey. He has seen how much my walk with God has been strengthened and he is aware of the huge role he plays in that.

If I had to give those reading this a piece of advice, it is to just listen to God when He puts people into your life, and do not be so quick to place them in a box. I was convinced that Clint's place was to bring me closer to God vocally, through worship music, which was not the case at all. Clint's voice is what got my attention, but His voice through Clint is what matters most. Be open to all God has in store for you.

Clint is just one of the men of God that I have in my life that constantly lift me up, celebrate with me, mourn with me, pray over me and are there for me. There are others like Pastor Mike Lee, David Siegel, Tommy Do, Phil Gallo, James Apap and the other guys I previously mentioned that have prepared me to lead.

They have built me up and gave me the confidence to become a men's small group leader. Now I have the privilege to co-lead a men's group every Tuesday night and also do social media for the larger men's community at Liquid. They say iron sharpens iron. Well, I will always have tools primed and ready with the people I have been lucky enough to have in my life.

I needed that support more than ever when my brother, Mark, unexpectedly died at 46 years old at the end of April. As I mentioned earlier, I lost my dad when I was 23 and I thought that would be the hardest loss I ever suffered. Unfortunately, that was not the case. Losing Mark so unexpectedly ripped our hearts out. As I write this, it has only been just over three months since he went home to God, but the wound has not even begun to heal. The nights are the worst for me because I constantly replay in my head the events of that morning.

It was a little before 6 a.m. when my mom's cell phone rang. I did not think anything of such an early call because she and my sister talk at least 300 times a day. But this was not a normal call. My sister was delivering the news that my brother's roommate had found him deceased on the couch watching television. The day that followed was a blur, yet is also crystal clear in my mind. To say that we were in shock, and still are, would be an understatement. I need to be healed more before I can go into depth with the enormity of what his loss has meant to my family and me.

What I will say about that day, is that I owe my brother-in-law Danny an eternity of gratitude for what he did for all of us. When the cops were called and showed up to where my brother was living, one of the officers noticed my nephews in a photo. They immediately knew they were my brother-in-law's sons and notified his police department. He was not working, so one of his guys reached out to him to let him know. He had the unenviable task of telling my sister and my nephews, who were incredibly close to Mark, as was my brother-in-law.

Once they all arrived at my house, my mom went over to my brother's home with Danny so she could hold Mark's hand until the coroner came. That entire process took close to three hours. Once Danny knew the medical examiner was almost there, he had his friend bring my mother back home. He then stayed there until everything was over and probably went through emotions we will never know and saw things we would not want to.

I sit here typing this and cannot even believe it is reality, if I am being honest. The magnitude of the loss is felt every day. It is something I am still processing, but the one thing I do know for certain is that my brother is finally at peace. He is with our dad and our Father for eternity and I look forward to the day we are all reunited as a family.

Two weeks after my brother's passing and one week after his burial, it was time to say goodbye to my best friend, Ripley. I have always been close with our dogs because they are just full of unconditional love and you are their whole world. I was not ready to let go of Ripley that day, and quite honestly, I never would be.

Ripley had been diagnosed with PLE (protein-losing enteropathy) in July of 2020 and spent time in an animal hospital. PLE is an intestinal disease where the absorption of protein and other nutrients is extremely impaired. What followed was two years of endless prescription medications, prescription food and prescription treats. He had to go for blood work every month to make sure his levels were good. There were months they were okay and there were months where they were so low, we thought it might be the end.

But he fought on like a champ and was loved and cared for so much that he kept fighting. He had just gotten a clean lab report when he developed an eye infection. We tried drops, salves, more prescriptions and it was not clearing up. We brought him to the animal hospital and the vet did not give us good news. We were still reeling from the loss of my brother and were faced with a decision no pet owner wants to make. The outcomes of surgery were not good, with the likelihood of his eye having to be removed. The time had come to let this strong fighter enter God's kingdom. He was so tired of fighting and was not himself anymore. He was ready and although we would never have been, we did what was best for him. It was like throwing salt into an already gaping wound.

You see, Ripley was the dog who was with me through all of my ups and downs with my mental health. He was my constant companion. There were no expectations from him other than to be loved and cared for. I always would say I loved him and my nephews, Danny and Cameron, more than any other souls on this side of Heaven, and I meant it.

All this to say, the old Bryan, the hurt Bryan, would have raged against God for these two back-to-back tragedies. Do I have questions? Absolutely. Does it hurt? 100 percent, every day. But my faith in God is at such an all-time high that I know His plan and the things that happen on this side of Heaven are not always things we expect or want. We may not welcome it, we may not want it, we may not have asked for it, but He knows we can handle it.

I can tell you without any shadow of a doubt that I would not have been able to get to this place of acceptance so quickly had it not been for the people I surround myself with at Liquid Church. I have been raised up, loved and cared for so well, and that has given me the strength to fight on and not get wrapped up in the enormity of the two losses. The stronger I can be for myself, the stronger I can be for my family. That was something Mark taught me. He took up the "man of the house" title after my father passed, even though I was the oldest. I do not mean financially, but just being the strong one, even when he was suffering. It is something I will always admire about him.

I would like to address the proverbial elephant in the room for those who have known me longer than two years. I have had so much growth over these last two years that sometimes I do not even recognize myself or how I react to situations. But I will say I am proud of the man I have become.

That is a different definition and sense of pride that I was feeling while I was wrapping up my first book. I had been putting all of my focus on my identity on the horizontal and not on the vertical. I put all that I had and all that I was into being this sarcastic, gay, lovable guy. My pride came from being part of a community that has had to (and still does) fight for equality. That fight has not been easy for myself and many others, nor was it easy for the majority of my adolescence and adult life. Being gay was not as accepted and talked openly about when I was growing up.

By the time I was in college, I was out (except to family), loud and proud, but I never felt complete. I was always chasing something. I never felt settled. I was always trying to fit in, much like I had been during my youth, when I was bullied, sexually and physically abused. I did things I was not proud of and brought me shame. I knew God loved me and always would, but I did not love myself. I am certain God sensed that and put me on the path to my true calling He has for my life.

The one constant has always been my heart to help people. Now that I have combined that with serving God, I am the best version of myself that I have ever been. Is it always easy? Nope. But nothing worth it in life ever is.

I have to be honest. The hardest thing for me is feeling like I am being a "sellout" to the LGBTQ+ community. But feelings are not facts. I take great pride in the way my relationship with God has been strengthened. But what I have learned is that God created us to love and honor His name and His son Jesus. Are there hurtful and hateful words being thrown at the LGBTQ+ community by Christians and vice versa? Without question. My journey has been met with love, kindness, encouragement, acceptance and prayer. Not because of the identity I set aside, but because of who I am in His eyes.

I wish I had a perfect answer to give to an LGBTQ+ person who feels attacked by Christians. But what I can say with 100 percent certainty is that you are loved, you are seen, you are enough, and you are welcome in God's house. If that last part does not ring true where you currently attend weekly services, please find a church that loves and welcomes all people. Find a church that does not "measure" sin and treats you with the love and kindness you deserve, and that God freely gives.

The LGBTQ+ community wants to be loved, truly supported and not feel like they are sinful trash. The way to reach people of any community is to love and lead like Jesus. In John 8:7, Jesus commands the people in the crowd who are without sin to throw the first stone at the adulterous woman. You know how many of them followed through? Zero. That's right, there was not a person in the crowd that was sinless. I am not, you are not, church leaders are not, Christians are not. If we all learned to love and live like Jesus, this world would be a far better place to live in.

Through Liquid Church I have met incredible people. There are too many to name individually and what they have contributed to my life. But through this church I am able to serve God, work with those less fortunate than I am, bring people closer to God and if it is in His plan for my life, I want to minister to others, the way I have been poured into. The different campuses of Liquid Church are just buildings. The heartbeat of Liquid Church is the people.

On the next pages you will read interviews with people who have touched my life in one way or another on my walk with God. There are pastors, mentors, worship musicians, those who are in the special needs community, those who lead the younger generation and those that are the next generation. There are even a few actors who agreed to share their walk, even though it does not always seem like Hollywood celebrates that. Dig in and be inspired by these people. Be open to their words and hearts.

Tim and Colleen Lucas

Bryan: Did you both come from homes that had God at the center of them?

Colleen: I grew up with my mom and she was coming from a Catholic background, but was not involved in the Catholic church at all. I had an exotic childhood insofar as that it was an unusual ride. My mom met a guy in a band because she sang. He invited her to church, so we went to this Pentecostal Assemblies of God church in the Bronx. People were raising their hands, praising God, and speaking in tongues. At the time, I literally thought they were all freaks. I was so uncomfortable.

My only experience with church had been Catholicism. If you compare Assemblies of God to a Catholic church, they are opposite ends of the spectrum. I used to give my mom a hard time every Sunday like, "Why are you taking me to this freak church?" I was a teenager and having full-blown temper tantrums. But I grew to love the people, and they loved me and accepted me. Their love, over time, just melted my heart. I also saw a radical change in my mother. She went from being a wild child to being a mom, for the first time in my life.

Christ was the cause of that change, and I couldn't deny Christ. I ended up accepting Jesus when I was 12, and really, it had to do with the radical change in my mom's life. I'm like, "Clearly God exists. And clearly Jesus saves. I am feeling and living the difference that He's making every single day."

The services were literally all day long. Services would start at 9 a.m. and it was three hours of worship, until noon. We would go home for lunch and then come back for the evening service. I would say it was probably a good part of a year before I accepted being there, but I am so happy I did because it made all the difference in my life.

Bryan: How about you, Pastor Tim?

Tim: My upbringing was the opposite of Colleen. I grew up in the church. I can't remember a time that my parents didn't drag us to church. It was not charismatic. It was a small Bible church with very strong Bible teaching. There was not really much preaching, just teaching. I internalized early that, "Hmm. The Bible always has three points to it. And faith is you fill in the blanks". You have life, then there are problems, and God's word gives answers. It's like a recipe book, and you just fill it in, and so it was really boring to me.

I remember my dad would give me an allowance of $1, and he would give it to me in dimes because when we'd go to church, you always had to tithe. I would always have to put one of my dimes into the collection. From early on it was pay God first, and I appreciate that, looking back.

We learned the fundamentals, but you can imagine, for a 12-year-old kid, it came across as having to give my money away, always having to take notes, which I already did all day in school, so now there is more school. Then you sit in the big service and then we would go back to church at night and take more notes.

But I'm grateful for that now because that's where I learned a lot of the Bible. In fact, I wish that for more people, at some level. I remember being probably 16 or 17, and they would give you a program, and the notes would be the fill-in-the-blanks. We would go to the service, then during the hymns part, where everyone's singing, and before even hearing the message, I just filled in all the blanks because I could almost predict exactly what the preacher was going to say. I handed it down to my mom and I was like, "I'm done." She got very, very upset by that. But that's kind of where I tuned out.

Then when I went to college, even though I went to a Christian college, I didn't really understand the church as, "Hey, this is a place where lost people come, who have messed-up lives, and they're broken, and they can find Jesus, who can change them." I was like, "This is where religious people come. We have all the answers. And if I meet a broken person, I can help you fill in the blanks, too." Which is not helpful.

I met Colleen in college, and you can now clearly see we came from very different backgrounds. You know, I joke about it and call mine the "frozen chosen"… no emotions. Stand up, sit down, fill-in-the-blanks. Col was the "happy clappy" churchgoer. We would go to her service, which was three hours long, and just disorganized, and it was the opposite of filling in the blanks. I was like, "Is there even an outline here?"

But it was wonderful. It really was. I remember Pastor Mark then gave an altar call, and people came forward. And I'm like, "What is happening?" Because you would have people come in off the street.

Colleen: We would. And our church was very, very outreach-focused. We were out in the community almost every Saturday. We would go to the projects in the Bronx and help in any way we possibly could to anybody we possibly could. The breadth of our church was to do that.

When we started going to church together, it was very hard for us to find a church that had, Bible-wise, what Tim wanted in terms of the sermon, and then community, which is what I wanted. We both had that experience of what we wanted to bring. Trying to find a church that had both was hard.

Bryan: Tell me about how you met in college.

Colleen: We met in freshman writing class. Tim always jokes because it was late 80s/early 90s and I had big, big hair, and a very dark tan. He looks at me and said, "New Jersey. She looks like New Jersey." It felt like home to him when he saw me. Most of the other girls were from the Midwest, and they did not have big hair. They had beautiful, normal hair. Not the Aqua Net hair.

Bryan: What initially sparked your interest in each other?

Colleen: My roommate, Steph, was into hockey big time. Tim played on the hockey team, and they were a rowdy crowd. I just remember seeing him on the ice. He had long hair and he would take off his helmet at the end and flip his hair like a Breck shampoo commercial. He and I made eye contact because the rink was tiny, with a chain-link fence. I said to Steph, "I want to date that boy." Then, sure enough, would you believe he called me a couple weeks later and asked me on our first date. It was Halloween and I went dressed as a hockey player and he went dressed as Elvis. Appropriately so, we went ice skating.

Bryan: Where were you guys at in your faith journey at that point?

Colleen: I was very interested in church because I had this radical conversion experience. I had gone on mission trips and things like that. I was very interested in pursuing and deepening my faith.

Bryan: What was that like for you, doing the mission trips at such a young age?

Colleen: Growing up with a single mom, we really did not have a lot of money to speak of, so we didn't travel, or really do vacations. My first mission trip was with Teen World Outreach when I was a junior in high school and I went to Mexico. The letters I wrote home are so funny because all I wrote about was, "Oh, my goodness. There's nothing to eat here." I mean, I was clearly a child who had never been out of the country, and who did not do well with culture shock, but I loved it. It was an amazing experience.

Tim: You only have a few moments in your life that are cinematic. That moment at the hockey game was one of them.

To circle back to my spiritual journey, getting to know Colleen, and then her mom in this church that really did expect the Holy Spirit to move and do something unique each Sunday, was the opposite of a predictable outline. My church represented predictability, going through the motions, whereas there was a sense of expectation that God would do something new any moment.

I asked Colleen on our first date, and she infamously turned me down. I said, "You want to go out Friday night?" She said, "Oh, I'd love to. But you know what? I'm actually going to be in jail on Friday night." I've been turned down before, but I never heard that excuse. But she was going to do prison ministry every Friday night to tutor young women in their teens and 20s.

Colleen: It was a co-ed juvenile facility. It was a maximum-security prison for girls and a minimum-security prison for boys. I would go in every week, and tutor them, and just form relationships. The girl that I tutored, Chevette, had a little son that she named Marquis. And I can't make this up, but she was in for grand theft auto. She was special, and we formed a great relationship. I intended to stay out in Illinois and work for the prison system, but by the time they had offered me a position I had been back in New York, and Tim and I had started our life together.

Tim: That experience she had tutoring in prison gave me a vision that your life and your faith doesn't have to be privatized to just an hour on Sunday. Most people are out partying on Friday night in college and Colleen was going to do prison ministry and tutoring.

That planted the seed for what Liquid became because outreach is such a huge part of who we are. God taught that to me, through Colleen. I like to think on our best days, our church is out in the streets and not just in the seats.

I think that is a way that God also brings people together. He has lives intersect in ways that we wouldn't have known otherwise.

Bryan: So first came love, then came marriage?

Colleen: I do believe my husband broke up with me.

Bryan: You took a break?

Tim: Oh, stop.

Colleen: Yes, he took a break.

Tim: I wanted a break. I didn't say breakup. I just wanted a break.

Colleen: He took a break.

Bryan: You guys are like Ross and Rachel from *Friends*. "We were on a break."

Tim: I was miserable during that break. It was the worst three months of my life. I said, "What am I doing? What an idiot. Let me marry that girl." So, we got married.

After we got married, we were attending a church in New York, Redeemer Presbyterian Church, which is a wonderful church. It provides a good blend and exposed Colleen to Bible teachings by [theologian] Tim Keller, who is phenomenal. They also had a lot of outreaches and Colleen was involved in ministry at a home for girls.

We were living in New Jersey, so it was very hard to be substantively involved in the body life of the church during the week. So, we started going to a 150-year-old Baptist church. I had no vision for being a pastor, but starting a church, for sure. God "tricked" us into it. The senior pastor said, "Hey, you guys are young and married. You want to teach a Sunday school class for 20-somethings?" And my wife said, "How early do we have to be here?" That was the start of Liquid Church.

We threw out all the fill-in-the-blank Bible studies and said, "Can we talk real life?" There was a real hunger for that authenticity and the serving component, too. That Sunday school class started with eight people. Then suddenly it was 18, and then 50 people. We moved out of the church, because we ran out of space, a mile down the road to a tavern. That's when we started calling it Liquid. Not because of beer [*laughs*]. But that was really the genesis of us starting a refreshing church experience. People started bringing their non-Christian friends and coworkers. Colleen and I would do Liquid, and then we'd go back to the church. But one Sunday we felt like we wanted to stay at Liquid with our friends. I didn't realize it at the time, but it was kind of like how you start a church plant core group. That is how it began.

Bryan: What made you want to make Liquid nondenominational?

Tim: I think we are living in more of a post-denominational age. Those things used to be important to people. We wanted a welcoming environment, where anybody could come from any religious background or none at all. We called it Liquid because Living Water was so on-the-nose.

People were open to coming and seeing something new. Millington Baptist Church was our mother church. They are dear friends to this day. But they launched us out in 2000, and our first service was 2001, two weeks after 9/11, so there was a palpable hunger for people to come together.

Colleen: I own a transcription company, so I was working and raising kids, and Tim was doing Liquid. But they weren't separate because I believe that God calls two. I don't think he calls one. I was always there to support in any way I possibly could. I usually was there all day on Sundays with the kids, and meeting with people, and I led a small group. But I never worked at the church. It wasn't ever full immersion, where we were both 100 percent all Liquid, and that was really good for us.

Bryan: Do you feel Liquid grew organically or do you think it really exploded once you launched?

Tim: I think we've gone through certain periods of explosive growth. But what most people don't know is that we didn't have any intention of starting a church. We were just volunteering, trying to be like, "Hey, yeah, we could teach that class." Then it just kept growing.

Then we thought about what the next obstacle was to get to people who are far from God. That's what led us first to the tavern. We had church at night because people we were reaching out to were out partying on Saturday nights, so 9:30 on Sunday morning wasn't the right time for them.

It was very bumpy, especially in the beginning, because we had two children under the age of five when we started the church. Everything's new; new people, new groups, new teams, new worship, new sermons, all this stuff. I was very consumed with that because we wanted to see it succeed.

Colleen is super high-capacity, so she is working, but also being a mom for the kids, 24/7. I didn't balance it well. I didn't have good boundaries. I always told myself, "Oh, you know, well, once we get through the first small groups, then I'll be here. No, no, no. Once we get through Christmas, Easter ..." I would just kick the can. I didn't realize it was rationalizing.

That was my first real bout with burnout in ministry. Ministry had become my mistress, I guess, in a way. I was giving it my first fruits, my very best of my energy, and giving leftovers to my family. I have met so many pastors, and you see so many stories today of people blowing up their lives, especially church leaders. They're having an affair, or they're divorced or, you know, whatever it is. That stuff doesn't happen all at once. It's a series of small little compromises. I had to really repent. Repenting is not just telling her, "I'm sorry," but saying, "Hey, what actions do we have to take to change this?" With the help of a counselor, we took a machete to my schedule and said, "You know what? I'm only going to be out one night a week." I was getting guest speaking invitations, but we decided I would not do that until the kids are older, then we could reevaluate. That served us so well over those years.

Bryan: Did you feel like you had enough support to do everything that came with launching what would become a multisite church?

Tim: We never felt overwhelmed because God graciously brought other people into our lives, like Dave and Lois Brooks, who started the church with us. I had never done a budget. I don't even do my own budget at home, let alone a budget for a church. But Dave was like, "I can help with that." He brought along people in media, people in worship, who had strengths and gifts that I don't have. He kept building the team, which had been a profound impact on our lives as well.

Colleen: God has brought different people into our lives. We love feedback, and we like to take whatever wisdom we can from those who are ahead of us. God blessed us with a lot of people who were ahead of us and who would gently suggest things to us. One of the things that was suggested was just that we always continue to date.

Then we had that moment that Tim talked about, where he really took a machete to his schedule, really putting a stake in the ground and declaring his love for me and for our family. That was a very big moment for us, and really changed our relationship.

Bryan: Do you ever feel like you are put on a pedestal being the lead pastor of the church?

Colleen: I don't think anybody ever necessarily means to put you on a pedestal. They like what you're saying, or they relate to you, and then they start to elevate you. We do try to knock it down and remind everybody we're just regular people. It is one of the reasons I'm not comfortable on the platform on Sundays. I prefer to be one on one any day with somebody. I prefer to be close, look you in the eye and have a real conversation with you. I don't need to know you very well to tell you the things that are on my heart because I just want to be real. I think it's amazing when God calls a husband and wife like that, and they can both preach, and that's a special thing. I am more comfortable behind the scenes.

Bryan: You both make sure to go out to the lobby after each service to greet the guests as they exit. How important is that for you?

Tim: Col and I love to stand outside in the lobby for as long as people like, and talk with them, hear their stories, and pray for them. Those interactions are very meaningful to me. Everyone at Liquid is accessible. There are no tiers or inner circle.

Bryan: Have you always had a charismatic personality?

Tim: I have a big personality in some ways. People think I am highly extroverted, which I am, in that I enjoy people and I enjoy being in crowds. That never bothers me. But what's interesting is, and Col would tell you, is that I have a very introverted side. One Sunday you speak to a couple thousand people, then I need to go home and be very quiet for a while. That's how my batteries recharge. During the week, I don't see a ton of people. I spend at least two days before the message just interacting with my family, because writing the message requires a certain amount of energy and engagement level that is emotionally draining.

Bryan: Liquid Church is Bible-based, which society is not in lockstep with. What would you say to those Christians who see that as discriminatory?

Tim: Jesus had this incredible ability to be winsome and attractional toward the most sinful people in his culture, right? People were drawn toward him. Yet he didn't compromise truth.

It says in John that Jesus came from the Father full of grace, unconditional love, and acceptance. You don't have to change a thing for me to love you. But also full of truth that, "Hey, God is holy. And he does have standards for his children to act differently than the world. The world will not understand it."

It is grace and truth, it's not one or the other. It's both/and. At Liquid, love and accept all people. They don't have to convert, get baptized, lead a small group, nothing. We're just going to love you the way that you are, because God loves you the way you are. But he also loves you too much to let you stay that way. There are parts of each of us, gay, straight, Republican, Democrat, all these different things, that God wants to redeem. We've got people who are politically idolatrous in this church. God's working on that. We've got people who are sexually idolatrous. Heterosexual, homosexual, you name it, who at the end of the day, they believe their identity as a sexual being trumps being made in the image of Christ.

Our world is extremely polarizing. But the kingdom of God is extremely expansive. When we get to Heaven, God isn't going to ask you, "Republican, Democrat, gay, or straight?" or any of these divisive issues. He's going to say, "What did you do with my son, Jesus? Did you add something to Him? Or did you take away anything from Him?" The Bible is the rule for our faith and life.

I have no expectations that people who are outside the family of God would live according to the Bible. Why would they? They would look at this as some antiquated document that's culturally irrelevant, and times have changed.

Bryan: Has that changed the way you preach at all?

Tim: I feel like God's called me to be a bridge-builder between people who think they're at odds with each other, to stand in the middle. But the challenge of standing in the middle is that you get hit with rocks from both sides.

I have had people say that Liquid was too conservative because we talk about people not sleeping together before marriage. Others think we are too liberal because we talk about racial justice or our posture toward kids who are coming out as LGBTQ or transitioning.

Our posture is to love. We make a distinction between our posture toward people and our positions on issues. Most Christians you see in the news, they take hard line positions.

Because Liquid is a church where Jesus radically accepts everybody. Grace is our posture. But truth is our foundation. If you ask me about things, I'm not going to give you my political opinion, or what I think moralistically should be the right thing. I will tell you what God says, and we can explore why He says that. But I'm not going to twist your arm to accept that. And if you don't, I'm going to love you just the same, probably even more so.

Colleen: We are all works in process. God meets us where we're at, and He works through us. None of us can do it on our own, we all need Him.

Bryan: In my case, and I doubt that I am alone, being a member and working at Liquid Church has changed my life for the better. You have a great perspective on who is responsible for that.

Tim: We, as a church, can't change anybody. We have zero power. Nobody can change anybody's life because God is the one who has that true power. I just feel very humbled that I get a front row seat to what He's doing.

Colleen: It is humbling that God would use us. There are so many amazing people at Liquid who have amazing stories and amazing backgrounds. At times I ask, "Why us?"

Tim: Remember, God calls the donkey to speak and preach in the Old Testament. It's very humbling to know that you're called with a donkey, right? When I am writing my sermons, I always think of how to impact the flock that He entrusted to us. We want to feed them a balanced diet of biblical truth, but also tend to their wounds and their hurts, challenges. It is like being a parent, but on a much larger scale.

I believe good biblical preaching should comfort the afflicted and afflict the comfortable.

Tim Lucas and his wife, Colleen, started Liquid Church in 2007 while meeting with friends in the basement of a 150-year old church. Tim is now the Lead Pastor. Liquid Church has seven campuses across New Jersey with a vision to "Saturate the State with the Gospel of Jesus Christ." Tim authored the book Liquid Church: 6 Powerful Currents to Saturate Your City for Christ, which is available for purchase on Amazon.com. Colleen is the CEO of Trans©ript (www.tscripts.com/). They have two children, Chase and Walker "Del". Instagram: @pastortimlucas @liquidchurch

Bryan: What was your relationship with God throughout your early childhood and how did your parents influence that?

Kayra: I was raised in a Christian household. My go-to joke is I was born on a Tuesday late for a prayer meeting! My parents have probably been the biggest influencers of my Christian walk and continue to be key pieces in my discipleship with Jesus. Like most people, I've gone through ups and downs in my relationship with Jesus…growing most in a steady relationship later on in my adult years.

Bryan: Growing up, when did you lean on Him the most?

Kayra: I can't remember a specific instance that I leaned on Him the most, but I definitely did throughout my teenage years probably the most.

Bryan: Was there ever a time that you didn't feel He was listening, and you questioned your faith?

Kayra: Yes, I have been in spiritual deserts, where the absence of God has been a prevalent feeling more than His presence. It's never made me question my faith…but I have felt dry in my prayer life.

Bryan: If so, how did you overcome that?

Kayra: By returning to the spiritual discipline of prayer and stillness.

Bryan: When did the idea of becoming a pastor pique your interest?

Kayra: Funny that I never thought about becoming a pastor. I've always loved the local church and have believed that the single biggest influencer to changing the world is the church. I have always wanted to serve in the church, but didn't think necessarily about becoming a pastor. It wasn't until I started working in ministry full time and that Liquid approached me with the opportunity to be the Campus Pastor of one of our locations, that I felt God stirring me in that direction.

Bryan: Your background is in law, and you were a practicing lawyer in Puerto Rico. What made you switch careers?

Kayra: How many lawyers do you know that are happy being lawyers?

Bryan: What led you to Liquid and what was your evolution from the start to now, as the Pastor of Campuses?

Kayra: When our family moved to NJ, we began looking for a church. A friend I ran into at the library recommended Liquid and when we came, we saw their hearts for the special needs population. Since our youngest son has Down syndrome, we knew we had found a home. Later, I started volunteering on the Spanish Translation Team, then became volunteer staff. Then part-time staff working in our Family Ministry, then full time as the Campus Coordinator, overseeing Sunday Service Logistics and Teams. Then pastoral staff when I became the Campus Pastor in Morris, and then finally, as part of our senior executive leadership team.

Bryan: What challenges presented themselves on your journey to being a female pastor?

Kayra: Some men have had a hard time thinking I had anything to share with them from a pastoral perspective...but some women have also said the same, particularly women who have been told their entire lives that they can't be pastors.

Bryan: How did you overcome those?

Kayra: It doesn't really bother me because I grew up in a church (back home in PR) where women were preachers and pastors, so I have never doubted once that I can do those things as well and that God has gifted me with those gifts. It helps me listen to people who have had other experiences and empathize with them without getting defensive.

Bryan: Many who are fortunate to know you at Liquid have been blessed by your encouragement, words of wisdom, mentorship, and guidance, whether they be on staff or members of the church. How do you handle the pressures that go along with that?

Kayra: I have two kids who love to make fun of me and keep me very humble, and a husband who is my best friend, but who also doesn't shy away from speaking the truth in love!

Bryan: Who inspires you?

Kayra: I think the staff at Liquid inspires me. We work with some of the most gifted and talented leaders in the Northeast. I learn from them every day!

Bryan: God has blessed you with a beautiful family – husband José, daughter Gaby and son Andy. Your son Andy, who has Down syndrome, led you to move to the States. How difficult was that to uproot your family, career, and entire life, albeit for the best possible reason, which was to get the best health care possible for your son?

Kayra: Probably the biggest earthquake event we have gone through as a family. It is very painful to live far from family and to be alone at times on major holidays if we can't travel back home. Our family is very close-knit, so I do mourn the fact that my parents are not in our day-to-day lives in the way that they were when we used to live in PR.

Bryan: You will be married to José for 19 years when the book comes out. What has been the keys to the success of your marriage? How did you both overcome the challenges put on the marriage?

Kayra: I think the fact that we are great friends…we have a lot of things in common, but also that we laugh a lot together and don't take ourselves too seriously has been tremendously helpful! I've often thought God's grace for me is shown through the ways in which my quiet and patient husband puts up with me and all of my warts.

Bryan: Anyone who knows you, knows that Gaby and Andy are your pride and joy. Can you describe what makes each of them special and the things they have taught you?

Kayra: From my son Andy, I've learned what it means to wash people's feet. [Because] he has Down syndrome and quite literally cannot put on his own shoes, every morning, I bend down and serve him by putting his shoes on. God reminds me that I'm washing my son's feet in those moments. He has taught me to love people for who they are, not for what they can do.

From my daughter Gaby, I've learned to become a better observer of people. She is a sensitive and introverted soul who is incredibly perceptive and very insightful in her observations about people and dynamics as a whole. I've learned to pay better attention to those things. And humor…she's incredibly witty and has a dry sense of humor.

Bryan: What is the most important lesson God has brought to your attention so far on your walk with Him?

Kayra: How broken I am and how far I still have to go. Who I am becoming is more important than where I am going.

Bryan: Finally, what is your advice to those who want to become a pastor and use their servant's heart to spread His word?

Kayra: Keep saying yes to serving Jesus and doing well with the opportunities He presents. Don't think you have to ask for it or fight for it. The Lord will take care of all of that if that's His plan for your life.

Kayra serves as the Pastor of Campuses at Liquid Church. She relocated from Puerto Rico to New Jersey in 2012 with her husband, Jose, to get the best care for her son, Andy, who has Down syndrome. The couple also share a daughter, Gaby. Kayra has a law background and worked as an attorney for nearly a decade. Instagram: @kayrada

Bryan: What was your early relationship with God growing up and were you raised in a spiritual household?

Justin: My parents were Catholic growing up. They were divorced when I was seven. And for me, spirituality was not a central part of my life.

We would attend church occasionally, but if you asked me if I had a relationship with God, I certainly did not. If you asked me if I understood the truth of the gospel, I had no clue. When I was 13, my dad brought me to a Pentecostal church in downtown New Haven, Connecticut, called Church on the Rock.

Pastor Todd Foster gave a simple presentation of the gospel, and I was stunned. Almost overnight everything in my life changed and I opened my life to Christ. I experienced the presence and the power of the Holy Spirit in a way that was just life-shaping, and instantly the direction and the focus of my whole life shifted on a dime my freshman year in high school.

That was the beginning of my faith journey. My dad had just recently opened his life to Christ. We were kind of experiencing God right around the same time.

Bryan: Did that bring you guys closer?

Justin: Yeah, I think so. It was a tricky time for us as a family. My mom was getting remarried. My dad was getting remarried. I had a new stepbrother getting introduced into the equation.

Freshman year is the beginning of your formative years and leaning into God is not a very "cool" thing to be into. For me, it was a transformative time. I was just starting to date a girl that I had liked since the fifth grade. She was not following Jesus. That relationship did not go well because I became a Christian. Everything about me was just changing so quickly that after a few months it was like, "We're heading in completely different directions." I played basketball at the time. My friends on the basketball team did not understand why I was at church every day that I could get there. They did not understand what was going on with me. And truthfully, I didn't really understand it, either.

The first couple years of following Jesus were tough for me. I was a failing Christian. I was deeply in love with Jesus, but I was always tangled up in some sin, always feeling like I wasn't good enough. I didn't really understand grace. It was hard. I experienced the power of God, but I had a lot of untangling to do before I experienced the joy or the peace of God on a consistent basis. Like a lot of people, I came to Jesus, and I came with all my mess, and He has been untangling me ever since. But those first couple years were tough.

Bryan: Did you have anybody that mentored you in that time to get you to where you are today?

Justin: God was gracious to bring the right people at the right time. I think if most of us look back at our stories, we find that God has this plan. For me, the first person was my youth pastor, Rick. He used to meet with me at Dunkin' Donuts at 5 a.m. Each week we would study the Bible together. That was huge, for me, freshman year, sophomore year, those formative times. He gave me opportunities to lead when I really didn't deserve it. He took a risk on me and gave me opportunities to lead worship. I was in a band at the time. I had been playing music since I was a little kid.

He gave me space to try those things out. Eventually, he gave me a chance to preach. The lead pastor of our church, Todd Foster, took an interest in me and just made time for me. At the time, the father of the drummer in my band, Brian Simmons, was the pastor of another church.

I remember going to his house, and I had never seen so many Christian books everywhere. I was thinking, "This is nuts." My friend told me I could take whatever books I wanted, saying, "My dad loves to give books away." I took so many books after I asked him if he was sure I could have them. Then his dad came downstairs and greeted me. I was like, "I'm just taking your books." He gave me one book after another to take.

That was really formative for me. I'm grateful that I felt right away that God started intersecting the streams of Christianity. I grew up in a very liturgical Catholic experience, but we weren't very consistent. I then had a Pentecostal experience, which had long services, lots of expressive worship, and was very multicultural. And then from there, somebody gave me Bill Bright's *A Handbook for Christian Maturity* and *Bill Bright & Campus Crusade for Christ*. A lot of my formative biblical thinking started with those books.

Then I got involved with a Vineyard Church and really started to see evangelicalism and a charismatic church coming together and what that looked like. When we started traveling with this worship group I was with, we started working with the Southern Baptists and connecting with Methodists and Presbyterians. I never saw the body of Christ as this competitive, argumentative thing. I just was fascinated by the differences and celebrated them. So, by the time I was 23 or 24, I had experienced more diversity in my church than the vast majority of people ever do. That was a gift. That was a blessing, looking back. That was part of God's plan for sure.

Bryan: Were you ever on a worship team since you were in a band? Did you go out on tour?

Justin: I was part of a band in middle school. My dad is a musician. I started playing guitar when I was four or five. I was in bands all throughout growing up.

When I became a Christian, my youth pastor found out that I played guitar and asked me to go on this tour. I was 15 and went with our youth group band. That was awesome. I played guitar. One day our singer was sick, and he asked me if I could sing. And I was like, "Not really." And he replied, "Well, you're going to sing." I led worship that day and God moved really powerfully. My singing wasn't great, but the power of God was. He came up to me after and said, "Hey, you're the new singer." I was like, "*I'm the new singer?*"

Things kind of took off from there. I did that through college. This is going back to the '90s. The band was originally called Holy Fire. We were a youth group band that just kind of exploded. When I got out of college, I started a new band called Out of Hiding. We traveled full-time for seven years after college, all over the world, leading worship and preaching. We did over 130 events a year, all through our 20s. My wife, Chrisy, was the keyboard player.

Bryan: Is that how you guys met?

Justin: We had a mutual friend who left for Youth with a Mission's discipleship school, and we met at a going away party. Our birthdays are 10 days apart and we were about to turn 16. We were kids. We've been married 17 years, but we've been together 23.

Bryan: Did being on stage and leading worship, being in the band, make you more comfortable when you eventually started preaching on stage?

Justin: It is funny and awkward how we stumble into our gifts. I never saw myself as a preacher. I really didn't even see myself as a singer. I liked writing music, but I always knew that my strongest gift was leading people to worship Jesus. But the more I led worship, the more I felt this burning call to share things that God was speaking in my heart. Pretty soon I was talking more than I was singing, and people would say, "Aren't you guys supposed to be leading us in songs?"

Within a couple years of me leading worship, people started asking me to preach. I went to a ministry school where some of the leaders of the school had prayed for me. One of the pastors said, "Hey, you're going to preach." I remember thinking, "I don't know if I'm going to preach. That's not really what I do."

I am kind of an introvert by nature. People sometimes don't think that now because I'm a preacher, but naturally I just didn't see myself preaching. So, I struggled with that. Our band just kept getting invitations for me to speak at things. That is how I started preaching.

Bryan: When did you decide you wanted to go into ministry.

Justin: Out of high school, I knew I wanted to go into ministry. I wanted to get a degree at some type of ministry school. I had done really well in high school, and I liked school. School in particular was one of the great tests of my life. I tell this story a lot, but I was on the top level of a double-decker bus in Chicago preparing to commit to go to Moody Bible Institute as a senior in high school. The Holy Spirit spoke so clearly to me and said, "I do not want you to go here. I want you to stay in Connecticut and learn how to make disciples." I remember thinking, "Stay in Connecticut? There's not a single school in Connecticut that I even want to go to."

A couple weeks later, I got a letter from Southern Connecticut State University offering me a full scholarship for academics to do whatever I wanted to do. I threw it away because I was like, "There is nothing at Southern I even want to go to school for." My dad pulled it out of the trash and said, "Justin, would you at least just think about this?" So, I met with my pastor and talked with him. I knew I needed to stay in Connecticut. I felt like God had spoken that to my heart. I was in the middle of helping my youth pastor plant a church in Connecticut. I thought, "This will be a good experience for me." I was part of his leadership team. He said to me, "If you go to Southern and get a degree, I'll do a four-year apprenticeship with you. At the end of that apprenticeship, I'll license you for ministry." I ended up getting a degree in social work and was licensed for ministry over the course of those four years.

I started a nonprofit traveling ministry. I did that for four more years but stayed in leadership at my church. My church came back to me and said, "We want to ordain you." We're a nondenominational church, but licensing was something that didn't travel with you outside of the church. Whereas ordination was something that you were now legally allowed to ordain others and license others. That was my introduction to ministry. A degree in social work was the degree that made the most sense within the context of where I was heading.

There is another side to the story, which was that I started leading guys to Christ my freshman year. I led the running back for the football team to Christ. We ended up moving in together, leading another guy on the football team to Jesus, and over 30 guys on the Southern Connecticut football team ended up coming to faith.

We saw the Holy Spirit move a little at that school. It was my introduction to making disciples. By my senior year, I was living with nine guys in a two-bedroom apartment, and we were making disciples. It was a jungle. It was a crash course in how to lead people to Jesus and grow them up in faith, and it was awesome. I wouldn't take it back for anything. It was a great experience.

I knew I was called to ministry, and I knew I was called to New England within the first couple years of coming to Jesus. By the time I was 16, I had written a vision. God called me to see spiritual awakening in the Northeast and that I was going to give myself to that. I did not think I was going to start churches, though, or that I was going to pastor churches, because at that time in the '90s, in my experience, church didn't seem to have the potential to make a significant impact. I hate to say that, but the churches I had looked at, about 99 percent of the churches in New England were declining. Most of them were less than 200 people. They were not relevant to culture. They were not reaching people. Evangelism was not effective. By and large, I was looking at the church thinking, "I don't want to do that."

So, we started this traveling music ministry, and with it we wrote books, we wrote songs, and we held youth conferences. We did college campus outreaches, we were seeing thousands of people meet Jesus, and it was awesome. It was only during that time, after things really grew, that we started getting invitations outside of New England. Now I am traveling the world at 26 or 27 years old. I felt this constant magnetic pull back to the Northeast. I was struggling with that, and I felt God really compelled me to read the Book of Acts until I felt a clear picture of his purpose. I read it over the course of months, more times than I can count.

This deep conviction started to grow in my heart that the local church was God's plan to reach cities, not a traveling music ministry, not college campus outreaches, not evangelistic campaigns, but the local church. That was Plan A and there really was no Plan B. If I wasn't planting churches or growing churches, I really wasn't aligned with the mission of Heaven and the plan of God. That was an incredibly uncomfortable idea for me at the time. And I struggled with it for a long time, and it all came to a head in 2010. We were opening for the Christian group Casting Crowns at a Six Flags in Virginia.

We finished our concert, and I walked off the stage said to my wife, "I think we're done." She asked me, "Done with what?" And I told her, "I think we're done with Christian music. I think we're done with the traveling band." She didn't want me to become a pastor. And I was like, "I think maybe we're supposed to start churches." Her dad was a pastor. She said that while she loved her dad, "I don't ever want to be a pastor." That was the beginning of the conversation. It took us another year and a half before we started a church. But that's where things started to shift for us.

Bryan: Did you and Chrisy have any kids while you were still touring?

Justin: Yes, our first son had been to 12 countries by the time he was two. We had a full-time nanny that traveled with us, and we had two boys on the road for the first five years of their lives.

It was an incredible way to spend our 20s. What I didn't realize at the time is that God was giving us a front row seat to how church happens across America and the world. We were getting to see the internal operations of local churches everywhere and seeing what the pros and cons were.

I don't think anyone has ever gotten such a view of the local church that we got serving the church. We would go in and do a big youth outreach and meet the pastor. I would preach on Sunday morning and then we would go to the next church and do the same thing. It was a sweet education for us, and we did it with our best friends.

There were about 10 of us that traveled. Five in the band, a person that did our merchandise, our nanny, our booking guy, and our kids, and it was awesome. It was a lot of fun. We learned a lot, grew a lot and we laughed a lot. It was a good time.

Bryan: Did you launch anything before Vox Church?

Justin: No, we didn't. I brought this to my wife. I brought it to our ministry. At the time, there was, I think, nine of us on staff. We all started praying, started reading the Book of Acts together, started asking God what He would have us do. We decided to do a church service Sunday morning in downtown New Haven on Easter Sunday 2011.

We weren't ready to start a church. We just were going to do a church service on Easter Sunday. We picked a famous, grimy dive bar called Toad's Place, right off Yale University's campus. It is a well-known bar, everybody from U2 to the Red Hot Chili Peppers to Snoop Dogg to Bob Dylan have played there. We did that church service Easter Sunday, and it caught like fire. I mean, it just exploded. It was on the front page of the newspaper. It was covered by *USA Today*, CNN, CBN. Everybody was talking about this church at Toad's Place.

People were saying, "Hey, when is your next service? We're so excited." There were hundreds of people connected now that wanted to come. It took us from April until September before we started the church. We were doing Thursday night Bible studies that we kept going. In September 2011, we started meeting every week.

Bryan: Did you preach in-between at all on Sundays at that bar after that Easter Sunday?

Justin: Just that one time. We went back there a few times and did baptisms, but we didn't have weekly services there.

Bryan: Do you think part of the attraction was that you were younger and that you were ministering to the college age crowd because you were by Yale?

Justin: Definitely. I think it was also this great oxymoron, having church at Toad's Place. We did not realize it at the time, but it was like the impossible, you know what I mean? It was the very holy sanctuary of wickedness and college craziness turned into Jesus worshiping.

At the time, the student newspaper *The Yale Herald*, caught wind of it. I think that's why it got so crazy, because, probably three weeks before, *The Yale Herald* heard about our service, and they wrote a big article that was supportive of us. I think that's how the *New Haven Register*, the *Connecticut Post* and everybody else picked up the story, because they heard about it from the *Yale Herald* and showed up that Sunday.

Bryan: Once you started Vox, how long did it take before it really blew up? Did you have a steady following right from the beginning?

Justin: That first service was pretty explosive. There was probably just shy of 200 people there. But for us it was like, "Wow, there are people here."

By the time we started in the fall, there was realistically maybe 70 that wanted to be a part of our church. That tripled in the first year or more. By the time we were a year old, we had a few hundred people, and we started our second location about 13 months after we started the church.

Bryan: That is quick after the launch of the first location, right?

Justin: Yes! It was 30 minutes away in the biggest city in Connecticut -- Bridgeport.

Bryan: You were the only pastor, so did you do live messages in both locations at different times?

Justin: No, the Holy Spirit spoke to my heart and told me that He had given me grace to do it on video. We bought a camera, and I asked my best friend, Cheech, who now runs a few of our churches, if he would be okay with me changing his garage into our new studio. He was my next-door neighbor. He agreed and we turned his garage into a studio. My buddy would film me, preaching my guts out Thursday afternoons in the garage with the squirrels running around on the roof. That was a problem. We'd be like, "Ah, you can hear the squirrels. We've got to get them off."

Bryan: At least you had an audience!

Justin: That's right [*laughs*]. We had no staff, and we had no budget. We would play that recorded video at the Bridgeport location. And 150 people showed up to be a part of it.

It was not a good plan. Three months in we realized, "Wow, first of all, there is a real church in Bridgeport now. There are over 100 people there. Second of all, we need to get a staff, like a pastor for that church, right away." We never launched a campus without a pastor again. But that first one, we just said, "Hey, let's give it a try." It was like the Idiot's Guide to Church Planting. I had never read a book on church planting. I had never sat through a seminar. I never went through an assessment. I wouldn't do it that way now. There are a lot of great assessments and books now. I would have used them if I had to do it over.

Bryan: How long before you got to the point where you said to yourself that you needed to add locations. Did it just happen organically because of a need in each of those areas that you opened locations in?

Justin: We always say, "We're a missional church." Our attitude is always, "We don't plant locations where people are coming from, we plant locations where people live." We find population centers and start churches. We had a pioneering, scrappy, grass-roots kind of a vibe when it came to church planting. We planted our third church the third year, in Meriden, Connecticut. It totally flopped.

Three months after we started there, only 30 people were attending. We shut it down and restarted it in Middletown, Connecticut. Attendance grew to a couple of hundred people quickly.

We went from Middletown to Hartford, from Hartford to North Haven, from North Haven to Stamford, from Stamford to Springfield, and from Springfield to Worcester, Massachusetts.

We kept spreading from there, opening one church location every year. Honestly, if it weren't for Covid, we would have 10 churches right now. We did decide to pump the breaks on one because of Covid.

Bryan: When you first started Vox Church, what were the initial beliefs, and have you had to change that because of culture shifts?

Justin: We really haven't. I had been studying the church at that point since I was 13, 14. And I had shaped in my spirit what type of church I sensed God calling us to start clearly from day one. We started on the three anchor values that are still the three anchor values today. They are – Jesus at the Center, Intentional Community, and City Mission.

We talk about them all the time and they are the bedrock philosophy of our ministry focus. Those three are the center of the gospel, Jesus living at the center. There is one name under Heaven by which we must be saved, and it is not the Father, and it's not the Holy Spirit, but it is Jesus Christ. That doesn't mean that Jesus is superior to Father or Holy Spirit. The Godhead is three equal persons, but the name of Jesus and the truth of what Christ accomplished is ultimately the doorway to salvation for all those who believe. How do I build my whole life on the revelation of the gospel and how do I allow that to then shape every aspect of who I am, my identity, the way I interact with God?

Gospel centrality is like an onion. You can always peel. There's always another layer. There's always another truth. The gospel is not something that we see as a message only for the unbeliever. Certainly, it is that, but just as much, it is a message for the believer. Every issue in my life is rooted in a lack of understanding or a lack of application of the gospel. The more I understand the gospel, the more everything else in life makes sense. Gospel centrality is our first value.

The second is Intentional Community. It's a deep conviction that I cannot know God if I don't know Him in and through my brother. Community is not a secondary issue in the kingdom. God himself is relationship. That's why He is triune. He is three-in-one at the center of the universe. Everything must come through and live through relationship.

Our third is what we call City Mission. We are going to go where people are. We are not called to be a pond. It is not a come and see; it is a go and tell. We are always on a mission to launch anything that would draw people to the truth of God's grace in their own lives.

Bryan: There are also so many different societal issues like racism, gender identity, sexuality that come into play. How do you love well but also stick to the Bible's teachings?

Justin: We are always seeking first to be defined by our love for one another. I would say that spiritual maturity is growth in agape love. That is the definition of what it means to be mature. I want to be open-handed to every person, and the *Imago Dei*, the revelation of the image of God, is definitely the driving force behind the acceptance of all people.

That is then married to the reality of the Lordship of Jesus Christ. It has been said that there's always two thieves on the sides of the Cross. One side is religion, the other side is irreligion. One side says, "Earn your way"; the other side says, "Make up your own way." There are always these two tensions. The "cure" for religion is grace. This unmarried, undeserved favor, that's given to all those who believe.

Also, consider the kindness of God stretching out his hands to us, and that the cure for irreligion is the Lordship of Jesus Christ. That considering his kindness toward us, you give him everything, sell all that you have and follow him. Let him become the king of your heart and the ruler of every decision in your life. Deny yourself, take up your cross and follow Him. I think that for us, we are always standing in the tension, we are right where the Cross is.

We stand in the tension of saying, "Hey, listen, we are going to love people radically. So, I don't care who it is." We just dramatically, passionately, wholeheartedly love them. We are going to love everybody, and we are going to love them with a radical Jesus type of love.

That's the one hand, this truth of grace. Then with that, we are going to teach the Lordship of Jesus Christ. We are going to hold to a radical commitment to Christ and a wholehearted devotion to Him. We are going to define sin as scripture defines it, even when it's really uncomfortable for our culture. I think that is the salt of the earth, right?

Most people are either legalistic, demanding, and condemning sin, or they are so gentle and loving that they don't really believe in anything.

The Cross is this incredible justice and mercy. It is kindness and love of God and the radical devotion to Christ. It is not one or the other, it is both. It is the perfect solution for the human condition. Modeling that is what causes the world to stand back and go, "But wait, aren't you supposed to hate me?" Or "Why do you love me better than my friends love me?" That is the tension of the Cross.

Bryan: How do you mentor them well, where it doesn't seem like you're forcing them to change, to adapt to being in a church?

Justin: I think the way that God works in our lives -- and I know for me it completely reorients my identity -- is so beautiful and uncomfortable and healing, and it is hard. Sometimes it is really hard, right? People think, "Oh well, yeah, I just changed." Not exactly. I know for me, since I was young, I was bound up in sexual temptation and sin and my thinking. It took a long time for God to rewire my soul, to change the way I looked at women, to change the way I looked at myself, and change the way I valued my appearance. And thank God I am still in the process. But there has been a freedom that's completely changed my life for years and years now. His ways are just higher than our ways. But I don't think there is any easy answer to that tension of grace and truth. I think that the best way to experience it or describe it is to live it.

I think every Christian is going to experience significant temptation. And I know, for me, I fight sin. I think for me, there was a huge change in my experience when the gospel was directly applied to my fight against sin.

Romans 6 was the turning point for me. Sometimes you read the Bible and you read something and you're like, "There's something there." But you can't really articulate what it is yet. I knew it in my heart, but I didn't have it yet in my head. And so, during a time in my life years ago, I memorized the whole chapter of Romans 6. I was just trying to get it in my mind and let the truth supersede the truth of my temptation.

I experienced at that time a real shift in how I fought sin because Paul talks about it when he says that your old self was crucified with Christ and that it died.

So, sin no longer has authority over you because its rule in your life ended with the death of Christ. I've been identified with Christ in such a way that now sin's power has been severed. Just like a marriage ends upon the death of an individual in the marriage, so sin's marriage to my heart ended when Christ died because I was in Christ. Just as Christ rose from the dead, now I'm married to another. I'm married to the resurrection life of Jesus, so my true self is holy. My true self is free, even though I'm still living in the body of Adam with the nature of Jesus.

That tension is overcome when He says you consider yourself, or the old translation says, reckon yourself dead to sin and alive to Christ because sin will not be master over you anymore. Because you're not under law, you're under grace.

That was the shift. He says that now that you're under grace, you've been received by grace. You've been forgiven. You've been accepted. You are loved. It's not on your own merits, it's by trusting Christ alone. Because of that sure foundation, now you can access the resurrecting power of Jesus to walk away from sin and say, "No." And that shift in my mind changed everything. For me, things like lust, things like anxiety, fear, a lot of the things had been entrapments for me for years and years and years. Going in a cycle and feeling guilty and going through the same problems, finally were snapped. It wasn't like I was never tempted again. No, no, no. That's not how it happened. I'm still tempted on a regular basis. It was that I didn't have to surrender anymore. There was a power that was introduced that was stronger than the power of temptation.

It was when I realized grace gives me the power to be dead to sin and alive to Christ. And that truth became more real than the feelings and the urges that I felt. When that shift happened, it was like it turned the faucet off. And I was like, "Wow, I can say no."

Now I could still be an idiot and say, "Yes." Absolutely. But I now had a power beyond my own ability to say no. What I realize is that anytime God tells me no to anything that I want, it's always for my own joy.

He is not robbing me of joy. He is actually setting me up for greater joy. And so, the pleasure of the moment is a two on the scale. But the purpose of him saying no is so that he can give me a 20 on the scale, way beyond the pleasure of the moment. That's when his law shifted in my heart from a burden to carry, to a joy to embrace. I realized all throughout the Old Testament David is like, "I delight in your law. Your law is like honey in my mouth." And I'm like, "The law? Don't kill. Don't steal. How is that honey in his mouth?" It is because when I obey God, I experience a higher joy than when I obey my own desires.

What I realized is you cannot get to happiness directly, but you can get to happiness through holiness. When I embrace holiness, even when it's unnatural, I find on the other side of holiness is supernatural happiness.

That change, that whole process in my mind has been for me, the single greatest catalyst to growing in holiness.

Bryan: When the enemy is on your shoulder telling you that you're not good enough, or that you're preaching is not good enough, or you're not a good enough husband or good enough father, what do you do to combat that?

Justin: There are two or three things I do right away. One is I call a friend. I have several guys who are mentors in my life. Our whole Board of Directors are not just guys that fulfill positions in an organization. They are godly men who have mentored me and fathered me and walked with me. I will call and say, "Hey, would you pray with me? Because this is what I'm thinking, this is what I'm feeling." And I need to say it out loud because as soon as you name it, you tame it. There is a preacher thing for you [*laughs*]. But as soon as you say it out loud, "Man, I'm really struggling with this insecurity about my value." Boom. You say it out loud. It goes down. It doesn't have the same power anymore. That is one of the things I do right away.

Another thing I do is I rope my heart to a promise or sometimes multiple promises. I have a "my time with Jesus" folder. It is full of promises. It's full of promises in God's Word that I can turn to in moments, whatever it might be. When I was meditating this morning on the eyes of the Lord running to and fro, throughout the whole earth to give strong support to those whose heart is blameless toward Him. I was praying, "Lord, may my heart be blameless toward you. And I believe, I receive it right now. I believe that your eyes are on me to strongly support me today."

That is a promise that I can wrap my heart around and hold to because it's bigger than the reality I see. That has been, for me, one of my absolute, bedrock convictions, and it is that the Bible is God's spoken word and it's truer than anything else that's spoken over me.

Bryan: You spoke about mentors, who you still have to this day for you as a leader of a church. How does it feel being a mentor to others, whether they're walking in the doors of one of your locations, whether they found and watch you online, whether it's someone like me who met you one time and just knew that God put you in my path for a reason? Then on the flip side of that, how do you handle people who see you on a stage and start to idolize you and not God?

Justin: The apostle John says, "I have no greater joy than to see my children walking in the truth." I am a dad with four kids, and I don't even think he was talking about biological children. I think he was talking about spiritual children. Any time that I can make an investment in the life of another, John Piper calls it Christian Hedonism. John says, "I have no greater joy." And it's true. People think that gathering wealth will make you happy, when in fact giving it away will make you happier.

People think that getting your name in lights will make you happy, when actually seeing someone else succeed will make you happier. And parents know this instinctively, right? But oftentimes we don't translate it to other relationships in our lives. But like Jesus said, "It's more blessed to give than receive." He wasn't giving us a command. He was teaching us a way of life. And so, for me, any chance I get to invest in the faith of someone else makes me really happy.

That is what Paul said in Romans 1: "I just want to come to Rome to impart a spiritual gift in you. Not just for you for me, because it makes me happy to be able to bless."

I love that phrase, it's my pleasure. "Hey, thanks for serving me." "It's my pleasure. No, it really actually is my pleasure." There's more joy in investing in someone else than in hoarding for yourself. I think when it comes to being able to bless somebody else, it really is my joy.

I do think we live in a celebrity culture. What I do is I try to come in low. I just met with a bunch of our leaders the other day to brainstorm ways on how to dismantle celebrity culture. Because celebrity culture to a degree is unavoidable, right? Jesus was a celebrity. Paul was a celebrity.

But I think the key to dismantling the idolatry of celebrity culture is to overcome it with servant culture. That is what Jesus did, right? He said, "The greatest among you will be the servant of all." For us, that's all about keeping your hands in the dirt. In the church world, as your church expands, it's easy to keep your hands out of the dirt to put on white gloves, live in an ivory tower and just do the clean part of ministry.

For me, that means leading a core group with a bunch of young men and being in their lives. It means leading a community group with a bunch of new Christians and being in their lives. My wife and I, we do both of those things.

It means for us a big part of it was becoming foster parents and adopting our daughter out of a very complicated, very messy world from our hometown of New Haven, Connecticut. Her mom lives 20 minutes from here. We talk to her every couple of weeks. It's not like this clean adoption, this is messy. You must keep living the mess of faith and that's what Jesus did. And that's what Paul did. If you are not willing to keep your hands dirty and serve, then you've lost the heart of Christ and He responds to the humble. If you become proud, your ministry might grow, but the kingdom doesn't grow. The kingdom only grows by the blessed or the poor and theirs is the kingdom of heaven. If I'm not poor in spirit, you might grow an organization, but you're not going to grow the kingdom.

Bryan: You are also an author. What is the writing process like for you?

Justin: I wrote my first book when I was 25 and no one ever read it. It never sold any copies really, but it was a good process for me. Then I wrote another one at 28, another one at 32, another one at 35, but no one has ever read any of them.

I just published a book last year, *Bury Your Ordinary* [David C Cook, 2021] and people were like, "It's his first book?" And I was like, "Yeah, my first book." It's my first book that anybody ever read.

As an author, I feel like I can hopefully make a difference in someone's life through my writing. Genuinely, for me, I don't want to be an author. I want to be a pastor. I don't want to be a traveling kind of speaker with my books. I don't want a side ministry. I'm not against that for others. It's just not for me. For me, writing books has always been first about creating resources for our community, for our church and then inviting others to experience some of what God is doing among us, through those books, outside our church.

My motive around writing is to get the message to people and to be a blessing and to bless our church. The vast majority of copies are sold at our church, which means that 100 percent of the proceeds go back to our church.

Bryan: What is your message to the younger generation and even to your own children who are the future of the church?

Justin: When grace gets in me, all my insecurities dissolve, all my fears about the future dissolve. "Fear not I'm with you. Be not dismayed, I'm your God." Isaiah 41 says. That's my promise. Because Paul tells us that every promise in Christ is yes, and so that promise belongs to me. All the implications of grace allow the human heart to come fully alive. Any message to the next generation would begin with the profound, offensive, glorious, and liberating truth of grace. Let that truth sink in so deeply that the fact that you're loved by God changes every other part of who you are.

From there, respond with a radical commitment to the lordship of Jesus Christ. So, because he's given everything, all things are yours. He says about God, "If he gave us his own son, how will he not also with him freely give us everything." Like what an offensive idea that God would give us everything. He says, "The world is yours." He says, "All is yours. All things are yours." If these sweeping promises are true, the only rational response is a radical, humble, submitted devotion to the Lordship of Jesus. So, give him everything. Don't argue with him. Don't debate with him. This is not a democracy; this is a theocracy. Jesus owns everything. To me, that is my message: first you must let your heart take hold of grace and be liberated. Then as you do, respond with the Lordship of Christ, respond with radical surrender.

Bryan: How do you manage not burning out as a pastor?

Justin: There are a lot of pieces to that puzzle. It starts with your soul. It starts with your time alone with God. That is an anchor for me. Just spending that first hour in the morning every day with God alone is refueling.

I practice Sabbath, a 24-hour period to pause, pray and play. For me, that starts Friday at 5 p.m. and ends Saturday at 5 p.m. I am intentional and consistent. I make sure I invest time with my family and my kids on a consistent basis.

My friend, Lance, tells me, "You've got to take your calendar by the throat." I am very intentional with my calendar. That's a big part of it.

There is also a physical side. I exercise five days a week. I eat healthy. I sleep seven to eight hours a night. I am diligent with all those markers to keep myself healthy. And then, I pace myself when it comes to work. I can't save the world; Jesus must do that. I try to stay in my lane and embrace limits and not try to be what I can't be.

Justin is currently the Lead Pastor for Vox Church, which he and his wife, Chrisy, started with a small group of friends in 2011. Vox Church currently has eight locations in Connecticut and Massachusetts. He and Chrisy have four children. Justin has authored three books: The Sacred Us, just released on September 6, Bury Your Ordinary, and Astonishing, all available on Amazon.com. Instagram: @pastorjustinkendrick @vox.church

Bryan: Did you grow up in a household where Christianity was encouraged and at the forefront?

Rick: Let me begin to answer this question from my perspective that a Christian refers to a follower of Jesus Christ who may be Christian, Catholic or any other denomination of religion.

Growing up, I remember a strong Catholic influence, as my mother was and still is a true traditional Catholic through and through. Honestly, I did not know anything about the Christian faith in my early walk.

I recall going to a church on Sundays with my family as we all practiced Catholicism during this time. We attended St John's Cathedral in downtown Paterson, which was also one of the first Catholic schools I attended with my older sister. We would learn about Catholicism at home, school and at church.

Reflecting on the preteen years in my life, I believe that my mom was the one who really helped set a firm foundation early on. My mom would display her faith to us as certain situations or circumstances would arise. She always had a strong faith in Our Lord and Savior, and I am so grateful for her and credit her with where I am today spiritually.

Bryan: A lot of Christians rebel in their teen and young adult lives. Did you do that?

Rick: Thinking back to my early teen years, I remember being part of the Pentecostal Lighthouse Youth Group. Yes, that's correct, I went from Catholicism to the Pentecostal, which was my first exposure to another form of the Christian faith. This group really helped to keep me centered and grow further in my faith.

It would be in my later teen years, around 16 to 18, when I absolutely rebelled. I slowly stopped going to youth group and favored hanging with friends more and getting involved in certain circles, which ultimately led me to getting into trouble with my family and even the law. I made some bad decisions that I regretted at the time where my life seemed to be falling apart around me. However, now I believe that those years, as crazy as it felt then, were a sort of preparation of how to help others around me who may find themselves in similar situations today. These were the teen years where I would say that I fell out of my faith and fell more into the temptations of this world.

Bryan: What was one of the most challenging times during that period?

Rick: Losing the trust of my parents and certain close friends, accepting that I was at fault and owning up to the mistakes that I made during these teen years was a very challenging time for sure. Growing into a young adult was an eye-opening experience for me. Looking back now, I can say that I was a broken individual who thought I knew all I needed to about life when in fact I had a lot more to learn and a long way to go.

Bryan: When did you turn your life back toward God?

Rick: It wouldn't be until my late 20s and early 30s when I would slowly begin turning my life back toward God. I met my wife during this time and my journey back to Him would begin with her. We would occasionally go to church, mostly on big holidays like Easter and Christmas. Then came a time where we would constantly fight over our financial situation at home. That is when we found Liquid Church, which offered a course on assisting families struggling financially. Going through these classes is where we would find a new community that we felt comfortable being a part of. Our class moderators invited us to Liquid's Sunday service and we would begin to listen and study scripture. We also joined a small group and on May 15, 2015, we both gave our lives to Jesus!

Bryan: You now have a family and are raising your daughter to be strong in her faith. What are you and your wife doing to make sure Julia has that firm foundation?

Rick: Our daughter is on a similar journey as my wife and I in that she is learning about the Catholic and Christian faith as we had her doing before starting to attend Liquid. With that said, we are consistently reminding her that her faith walk is her journey and not ours. We display the importance of prayer, learning the Bible and maintaining faith in Our Lord and Savior no matter the circumstances before us. We hope that we are able to help her maintain a firm foundation while keeping in mind that only she can find her true identity in Christ.

Bryan: What situations in your personal and professional life has prayer been essential to getting through it?

Rick: In my professional life, prayer was shown to me by my co-workers. I would witness them praying over good situations and bad situations. I would absorb this practice into my work ethic, and it has truly assisted me in getting though some situations. Situations that would include having tough conversations with a co-worker or a volunteer. Prayer at work has also assisted me in getting spiritually centered before having to perform my duties and responsibilities in my role as a leader.

In my personal life, prayer has been very essential and impactful. One main situation is when my wife and I were on the verge of divorce. I found myself praying and asking others to pray over our family. I am happy to report that with a lot of prayer and marriage counseling, we are still together and have connected on another level as a couple. Prayer is essential in my life.

Bryan: In addition to your own family, you have a huge family at Liquid Church, where you are one of the leaders as the Service Programming Director. You lead with excellence and handle things in a calm manner. Why do you think that is an effective way to lead?

Rick: I am so thankful for the Liquid Family and feel so humbled to be able to serve as the Service Programming Director who oversees Sunday services at the broadcast location in Parsippany. This particular role can be a stressful one for sure with trying to create the best engaging and distraction-free experience for guests on Sunday mornings. I believe that I handle most things in a calm manner as I truly believe in surrendering all things to Our Heavenly Father. Knowing that God's got my back in all situations really helps to keep me calm, centered and focused. I find it a very effective way to lead as it helps to keep those around me feeling calm as well.

Bryan: It is no secret that you have made an enormous impact on me, and I know you have done the same with others. What does it mean to you to be considered a mentor by many?

Rick: I have to say that I am truly honored to be considered a mentor by you and by others at Liquid. I love having the opportunity to pour into those around me. I have had a few mentors during my time at Liquid and I feel that I have learned a lot that I am able to pass along to individuals that I serve alongside weekly. It's such an amazing feeling that I get to have a small part in helping to raise up the next generation of leaders.

Bryan: How important do you think it is to have Christian brothers in your life to hold you up, hold you accountable, be a sounding board and to love you?

Rick: Having Christian brothers in my life is very important. I love how we can come alongside one another in the good and in the bad times of our lives. I find it amazing that a group of men can be there for one another as a brother in Christ ready to be present, caring and loving toward one another no matter the situation.

Bryan: You have been a true Christian brother to me personally and have made me a better man and a better Christian, which I articulate often. Do you feel the impact that you make on people, myself included?

Rick: Thank you, Bryan, for the opportunity of being a true Christian brother to you and for sharing the impact you've experienced. I believe that I see the impact when I see fellow brothers and sisters in Christ getting into a deeper and closer relationship with our Father. I really find it important to help point individuals around me to Christ and this is where I can most see the impact.

Bryan: One of your strengths as a leader is that you also want to learn from those you lead. How important do you think that is for not only you, but for those serving with you?

Rick: I absolutely love learning from those around me. I always tell those that I serve with that I don't know everything and that I am learning from them as they are learning from me. I think it's very important for those around me to experience and understand that they are contributing to the overall growth of the team and that their feedback and input is heard and an important part of our DNA.

Bryan: You juggle many different balls in the air at one time. How do you keep yourself grounded and not get yourself weighed down with stress?

Rick: Great question, as this is something that I have struggled with over the years. Through the assistance of my family and the Liquid Staff, I have found a few ways to help accomplish this goal. It is through a morning routine of prayer, reading scripture, along with exercise that really helps me to deal with stress. Also remembering that being fully present and placing family first, really helps to keep me grounded and try to live a stress-free life.

Bryan: Who are some of your mentors and what have they taught you that really stuck with you?

Rick: Some of my mentors would include Cuyler Black, Ed Ramirez, Ben Stapley, Clint Taylor, Lauren Bercarich, Hyo Sil Siegel and Pastor Tim Lucas. Each of these individuals really poured into me as I settled into my new role at Liquid. They taught me how to be a better listener, how to be very clear and concise when communicating or when casting vision to others, how to execute a plan effectively and efficiently from beginning to end, and how to maintain boundaries to have a healthy work/life balance.

Bryan: What advice would you give to other leaders to be as effective in leadership as one can be?

Rick: Some advice that I would offer would be some of the things that I have learned over the years. First, I would say to try and be a good listener. Sometimes I find that I want to speak into a situation or circumstance before fully knowing everything that is involved. Next, I would say to be flexible. In my current role, there are times when I go into Sunday services with a plan, but that plan has to be changed on the fly. Keeping a flexible mindset allows me to adjust and adapt to anything that may come my way. Lastly, to remember that prayer works and is essential in our day to day walk.

Rick currently serves as the Service Programming Director at Liquid Church's broadcast campus in Parsippany, NJ. He and wife Cecy share a daughter, Julia.

Bryan: Who influenced you the most on your walk with God?

Tee: My mother is my biggest influencer when it comes to God. She kept me in church. I grew up in church and it's all I know. I come from a very religious background, and a strict one at that. There was no such thing as staying home when church was happening.

Bryan: Did you grow up under a certain denomination?

Tee: It was Pentecostal Holiness, where you are in church almost seven days a week. Every Sunday, you went to Sunday school and then worship. Sometimes worship did not start until noon, and you might not get out until 4 if the Holy Spirit hit. Then you have to come back for night services, which started at 8, which could go as late as midnight.

Bryan: Was there a point that you started to want to distance yourself from church?

Tee: I left home when I was 16 and also left the church. In the church I came from, you could not do anything. You could not wear pants, earrings, or a chain around your neck unless it had a cross on it. Even in that instance, Jesus could not be on the cross. You could not go to movies. As a kid I lived in a strict household, and there was a lot of things I couldn't do. If I did want to do anything, I snuck and did it. That was a miserable way to live as a kid. When I got older, I departed, not from God, but from the church itself, and my home.

Bryan: Did doing that raise issues with your parents?

Tee: It raised issues with my mother. I don't think my dad cared. My father believed in God, but he was never one that went to church with us. It was always me and my mother.

When I was 16, my mother gave me an ultimatum. I was at a music studio one night and came home about 3 a.m. My mom's thing was, "My rules, my house, my way. You decide. Either you come here at a decent hour, or you leave and go wherever you are going". I chose to move out that day, and never went back.

Bryan: But that didn't make your walk with God any different?

Tee: I did drift away. I was able to do things that I wanted to do without somebody being over my shoulder. Even though God is still there, you don't think about that as a young person. I started smoking and drinking. I started hanging out at clubs, and all that other stuff that I could not do. I always felt funny doing it, because people would literally look at me and say, "You aren't supposed to be out here". So, there was always something, a call in my life, so to speak.

Bryan: When did you come back to the church?

Tee: When I was 17 after a year out there, doing my thing. When I was 17, one of my godmothers saw me and was like, "You need to come back to church." And I was like, "Mm, yeah, no, I don't think so." And she was like, "Oh, come back to church." And I said, "No, I don't want to come back to church, because I don't want to deal with all those religious people," which is how I referred to them.

She convinced me to come that Sunday after we spoke. Of course, the person that was preaching said everything that I think I did not want to hear, but I heard it. They made an altar call, and my godmother was like, "I want you to come to the altar for prayer." I did and rededicated my life to God.

I dialed back in, even though it was restrictive. Then I became miserable again, but I stuck with it. I knew that there was a calling in my life. I was always into preachers. I would soak up everything that they would say. I didn't always agree with what they said, but I took it all in. I really enjoyed women preachers because I wanted to do that. I wanted to be that person.

Bryan: Were there any female pastors you looked up to specifically?

Tee: Yes, Dr. Iona Locke, who is now deceased. [Gospel singer/evangelist] Dorinda Clark-Cole from the Clark Sisters was another woman I looked up to. I have been fortunate enough to meet both ladies.

Bryan: What led you to be a youth pastor?

Tee: I started off as an evangelist in the FBH, Fire Baptized Holiness movement. A "local evangelist" is what I was called. I had to go through training and all of that, and that's when I became ordained. And my pastor was like, "We need somebody to look after the youth."

I asked what it entailed. I was told to talk to God and ask Him for guidance on how to lead the youth at church and that is what I did. And I'm like, "What does that entail, really?" So, she was like, "I want you to talk to God and ask him for guidance on how to lead the youth here at the church. So that's what I did. And then I went to a youth pastor by the name of DeWayne Wright from Agape Family Worship Center in Rahway, NJ.

I was set up under his wing because he oversaw the ministry there. They had a huge congregation with hundreds of youths. I read a plethora of books, of course.

I became the Youth Pastor at Blessed Tabernacle Church in Elizabeth, NJ.

Bryan: How long were you a youth pastor and what made you step away?

Tee: I was a youth pastor for 19 years. My mom had a stroke which left her bedridden, which is when my life as a caregiver began. I was kind of being led away from youth ministry anyway. I was going to become an associate pastor in Atlanta. But that didn't pan out once my mother took ill.

Bryan: What do you feel you brought to the table for these young people, and now that you are no longer a youth pastor, have any of the people you pastored come back to tell you how much you meant to them?

Tee: A lot of the youth who came to our church did so without their parents, because they were working, some who didn't believe in God and others that were on drugs.

That is the kind of community I was in. I would bring these kids to my home. We would go out to eat. I was always feeding the kids, and rightfully so, because of the situation they were in. I have had to go to many court dates. I have had to go to many schools, sit and talk to the principal. Sometimes it would be me and not the parent.

Young people like to be heard. I know when I was growing up, that's all I ever wanted, was somebody to listen. I didn't always get that, so I gave things that I wished that I had had. I think if somebody would have talked to me the way that I talked to the young people in my youth, I wouldn't have ended up on the street.

Bryan: When you stepped away and moved out for that year, did you and your mom have the same relationship? Was she disappointed in you?

Tee: My mother was very disappointed. It never stopped me from loving her, but there was a big strain on our relationship. She wanted me in the church, but I wasn't comfortable. My mother stayed in that church, so I knew there was no sense going to their house, because she wasn't going to be there. She was going be at church. But I did keep in touch. My mother and I have always been tight. But it did put a damper on our relationship. When I found out I was adopted, then I came home.

Bryan: Did finding out you were adopted change your relationship with your parents?

Tee: Both of my parents were scared once I found out. My mother said, "Our fear was always that you would leave if you ever found out, that you would deny us and want nothing to do with us." It was the opposite. It didn't change how I viewed them. It changed how I viewed myself.

I found out by accident. Someone from the church told me, but they thought I already knew. Knowing that I was adopted helped me see my parents differently. I understood the hovering over me.

I'm glad I found out when I did. A part of me wished that I would have known earlier in life. But then again, I don't know if the way that I received it would have been any different. Hurt is hurt. I was hurt, regardless.

I didn't grow up in a household where there was punishment. I can't tell you that I've gotten hit or had beatings or anything like that. That was never my life. Oddly, I saw my friends get disciplined and wanted that, but I never received it and never understood why. I think my parents were afraid, because I wasn't biologically theirs, so they saw me as this precious gift they would not physically harm. Obviously not getting hit was a good thing physically, but mentally and emotionally, I'm not sure that was the right way to go.

Bryan: What were the feelings surrounding that from your point of view? Not that you felt like you were unloved, but did you feel a disconnect at times because you weren't getting hit?

Tee: I never felt disconnected from my mother, but I always felt a little distant from my dad. I would watch how he would treat his biological family, who I thought was my family. Like I could be talking to him, and the moment somebody else comes, he would totally ignore the fact that we were talking and start having full-blown conversations with other people and ignore me.

I always felt a little distant, even though he and I were close when I was growing up, too. I mean, he spoiled me. Like he gave me everything that I ever desired or asked for. Again, not sure if that was a good thing or not. But physically, he just wasn't there. He wasn't a typical father, like checking up on my boyfriends. He didn't do any of that. Often fathers ask who your friends are or where you were going. That was more my mother, not my pop.

Bryan: When you had to step away from being a pastor to care for your mom, did it cause you to stray from the church again?

Tee: I never strayed away from the church again. I just couldn't get to church, because physically I was helping my mother. She could not do anything for herself once she had taken ill, so I had to constantly be there. I think one of the things that hurt me the most at that time was with the church that I was attending. No one ever reached out to see if Tawana was okay.

It was all about if my mother was okay, and rightfully so. They should check up on her, but I mean, I'm a person, too. I'm going through it, just like her. Not in the same manner, but I'm putting in a lot of hours over here. I'm being mentally, emotionally, and spiritually drained.

But I had a relationship with God, so I kept it going. I know how to pray. I know how to read from my Bible. Thank God for the internet because I could watch sermons and be fed through that.

I ended up joining Liquid Church seven years ago, but didn't get involved serving/working there until four years ago. It is my safe place.

Bryan: What would you say to those people who do not understand the life of a caregiver?

Tee: Be mindful of what the caregiver goes through and that they are taken care of, because while they're taking care of those that they're overseeing, who's taking care of them? Especially when you talk about the church, right? If it wasn't for Liquid, and I'm just going be honest, I probably would've lost my mind in this situation.

You need a band of people that can stick with you and make sure that you're good, make sure that you're okay. The most important thing to me is when somebody says, "How are you doing"? Just knowing that you care that much, to ask how I'm doing is awesome.

A year after my mother's stroke, my father was diagnosed with prostate cancer and Dementia. That required me to be a caregiver on a whole new level. I lost a lot of friendships when my parents took ill because people couldn't understand that I can't be there like I used to. I am literally taking care of my parents. I have become their parent, so to speak. People did not understand why I couldn't just come to a party or pick up and travel across the world to go see someone, or for that matter, jump in my car and go three hours away. Especially not in the beginning. People were so used to me being there that the moment that I couldn't, they didn't think to be there for me.

Bryan: In addition to being a caregiver, and working, you also mentor many people. How do you keep all those plates spinning?

Tee: By not spreading myself too thin, because I have been down that road. I have learned balance. I talk to a lot of people. There are a lot of people that reach out to me, but I also have mentors and people that strengthen me, so that I can help strengthen someone else.

It means the world to me when the person can come back and say, "You know, I implemented the suggestion you gave," because you can't make anybody do anything. All you can do is just be honest with them. People love honesty. I love when people are honest, whether it's something that I don't want to hear or something I do.

If you're honest with me, we are good. Take time with people. As a mentor, I love just being there for people, just listening to their stories. I think if more people took the time to listen instead of trying to over-talk or out-talk an individual, you learn more. It's not always good to jump to conclusions about individuals. You'll know a lot if you just sit and listen and be observant.

Bryan: The youth today have different challenges than they did 20 years ago when you began your journey as one. Do you think you would pastor differently today versus then?

Tee: My style would be very different now. I'll always be truthful, though. I have no desire to be a youth pastor again, but I think that if more pastors, whether you be senior, younger, whatever, it doesn't matter, you have to learn the culture. You have to learn what's on these young people's minds and what/who are they listening to. The latest song or the latest gear or the latest anything, the latest sayings, how these young people talk. You know, you don't have to be them to reach them. You just have to know what it is that they're dealing with.

Get around young people. Listen to their conversations. Engage in what they're talking about and not be so quick to be that person that says, "Well, you aren't supposed to be doing this, that or the third." They know they're not supposed to.

I mean, I knew that, but I didn't want to hear that. I want you to hear how I feel. I want you to hear what I'm dealing with, what I'm up against. Because the generation that came before us did not go through what we are going through today.

They didn't have the type of world that we have on our shoulders. No generation goes through the same thing. Life repeats itself in certain areas, not in all. Don't be always so willing to only teach. Sometimes you can learn from young people. I think people miss that part, and I think why I stay so relevant with young people is because they know they can talk to me and I'm not going to judge them. I am never going to lie to them.

Bryan: I think that is one of your strengths as a mentor is that you don't pacify people or tell them only what they want to hear.

Tee: Pacifying people won't help anyone. I'm never going to tell you things just because it is what you want to hear. I am going be honest with you, because if I'm not honest with you now and then someone else comes along, you won't be able to handle that, you know what I'm saying?

You will always be accepted for telling the truth. People say they want to hear the truth, but they don't really want to hear the truth, right? A lot of people that I mentor have been upset with me for being honest, but then later, they come back and say, "I see what you were talking about."

Bryan: Some people can be a real pain in the ass to mentor.

Tee: Yes, you can, but anyway. But go ahead.

Bryan: Your chapter just got much shorter! How do you not throw up your hands and walk away when someone does not take all of what you say and apply it?

Tee: Because I am invested. Well, I think you should know me by now. I think you do know me by now. I don't just invest in everything and everyone. If I invest in you, I'm going to stick with you. We're going to ride till the wheels fall off, unless you just totally downright disrespect me. Then I'm gone.

The easy thing to do is just give up on someone. It is easy to say, "I'm done with it. You don't listen. Goodbye." But what good does that do? I think about the people that ended up in my life, that never gave up on me. My mother's one of them.

I'm 40-plus and I still have people who pour into me. Sometimes to them it may feel like I'm not listening, but I am. We are forever learning, and we are forever growing. Even though I'm mentoring others, it doesn't disqualify me from having to be mentored. What is shared with me builds me up so then I can help again.

Having a hand to help mentor you is a joy. One thing I can say about you, Bryan, is although you may not always be ready to agree with what I am advising you to do, you may even kick up against it. But after you have pondered it, you see it through a different lens. That's all a part of mentorship. It's a mentor's job to help guide you, but never to force you to go with what they've suggested. A mentor shows you the way, and it's up to the mentee to walk therein.

Bryan: Right, filled cups fill cups.

Tee: Build somebody else up. But yeah, to give up is easy. To hang in there is the hard thing.

Bryan: I feel "don't give up" could be a motto for your entire life and think that is part of who you are.

Tee: I don't give up. When I love you, I love you. I'm loyal, sometimes to a fault, but I am not that one to just walk away. I am a protector at heart.

Bryan: Everything you just said encapsulates our relationship and the heart that I see you have. What would you say to people who feel like they have that heart to mentor?

Tee: You can't be Jesus. I had to learn that you can't be everything to everybody. You have to know who you are assigned to, who you were called to, and the rest, be nice, but leave that alone. Whatever this gift that God has given me, many will refer to it as the "sermon." I know that is one of my strong gifts, but I get vibes from people.

If I'm around you or I'm communicating with you, sometimes you don't have to say anything. I'm just in your presence; I know whether to fool with you or not. I pick up like, "Mm, caution," you know? And then there are times when it's like, "We good to go," you know?

I always check myself. I always do a reflection, and I always pray, because I never want to assume anything about you or be suspect of anyone, because with the sermon, you have to be careful, because the enemy will play tricks and it will be an assumption and not the sermon.

You really have to be careful with that gift specifically. When I get cautious about somebody, I don't run to all these different people and say, "Stay away." I actually do go to God and [ask], "Am I to deal with this person? What's up with this individual?" Sometimes God will give me a direct answer, and then other times I've got to figure people will say, "Tee knows a lot of people. Oh, my God, Tee, you know everybody. And you talk to anybody." I do. I talk to everybody. And I will communicate with anyone. I get along with everybody. I just don't fool with everybody. There's a difference.

I don't open up to just anyone and everyone. I have select people that I am comfortable with. They've shown me that they can be trusted, not with my secrets, but with my heart. Because you have to make sure that people take care of your heart. I have that. Some of them are right here in this church.

I have to shout her out, Lady C [Colleen Lucas] being one of them. I love that lady.

Bryan: Absolutely. Both Colleen and Tim are wonderful people.

Tee: They have been a huge blessing. Grace Martoccia from the prayer team is another one.

Bryan: I don't think people fully grasp the concept of a church being a family sometimes, because they don't want to put in the time and the work that it takes to be in that family. But some of the greatest relationships you can have in your life, whether they end up being for better or for worse, God wanted you to be in that walk or with that person for whatever season it is. How important do you feel a church family is to you? When there's a member of that family who is a challenge to deal with, how do you navigate through that?

Tee: You take our church, Liquid Morris County has the largest campus out of all the campuses. Sometimes you can get lost in a place like this. But like I tell everyone, and I'll tell anyone, you come to a large facility like Liquid, you have to make the effort.

People will come and speak to you, but you have to put in the time to build relationships. Like I said, I've been going here for a long time. My first four years, I said nothing. I came at the 9 a.m. service and no one knew who I was. I didn't know a lot of people. It wasn't until I joined a small group that I built relationships. Once that happens, it starts to trickle down. My small group leader at the time, Kathy Szilezy, encouraged me to get on a dream team.

I was very reluctant because I'm like, "Do you know where I come from?" But at the time, I never shared that I had been a minister in the church. I never shared any of that when I first came to Liquid Church because I came here to be fed, not to be the one feeding.

But she encouraged me to join a small group. I did and I also joined Guest Connections. Then my world opened, because I started meeting the people I was serving with on Sundays which turned into relationships. And then from there, I went to Next Steps.

I would do Guest Connections and then I would do Next Steps. And then from there, I did both for a while, and then I got asked to do social media here, and it's all about connections, because you don't know who's connected to who.

This person introduces you to that person, and so forth and all of these relationships start to build. Now, you can't get close to everybody, but you can have real genuine relationships. When there is someone from your community who either strays away or there's conflict, I think as a church family, when you care, you go after that person. Find out what's going on, you know? Find out why aren't they coming. You don't have to get in everybody's business and make them feel bad, but again, Bryan, I can't stress it enough. People like to know that you care so just reach out. You're not going to get along with everybody all the time.

That's just the human side of us. But you don't have to lose a genuine relationship behind an argument or a disagreement or whatever. So yeah, genuine relationships in church are extremely important, because you all, for the most part, think the same. Each of you know how to pray, so you need that. You need people that will genuinely pray for you, whenever or whatever it is that you're dealing with or going through.

Tee currently serves as the Communications Coordinator for Liquid Church. Tee was formerly a youth pastor at Blessed Tabernacle Church in Elizabeth, NJ She is a mentor to many, a cherished daughter and the proud auntie to Carter and Bryson.

Cuyler Black

Bryan: When did your walk with God begin?

Cuyler: I was raised in the United Church of Canada. My father was an evangelical minister within an increasingly liberal denomination. He was considered by many to be one of Canada's best preachers. Before retiring, he served his last six years at the flagship church in the denomination, preaching to 2,000 people on Sundays. I grew up in big churches and loved listening to my dad preach. But faith isn't genetic. By the time I was in my early 20s, I had the head knowledge about Christianity, but I still hadn't yielded my heart. My parents displayed an attractive, vibrant, down-to-earth faith, but my self-centeredness overpowered any real surrender to Jesus.

Bryan: When did you realize being a pastor is what God called you to do in life?

Cuyler: I was dragged kicking and screaming by a friend to a church camp in my mid-20s. It was there that the walls of self-sufficiency and pride finally collapsed, and I realized that I wanted what so many of the 20-something and 30-something counselors and leaders at the church camp had – an honest, real trust in Jesus to lead their lives. On the bluffs overlooking a Lake Erie beach, I asked Jesus into my life. From that moment on, I felt integrated like never before. Reading scripture suddenly was like breathing fresh, clean air, and it made sense like never before.

I got very involved in the church camp scene there in southwestern Ontario, and eventually became a part-time youth pastor at an Anglican (Episcopal) church in London, Ontario. Basically, I just applied a lot of camp techniques and methodology to an urban setting. God grew that little youth group from 12 to 50 in less than two years. Two-thirds of those kids were low-income, single-parent, wrong-side-of-the-tracks kids, and I loved them. I was single then and so was able to pour a ton of time and relational energy into them. Those were great years.

I was also teaching at a high school. An offer came along from friends of my parents in Connecticut to come down and interview for a full-time youth pastor position at their church – another Episcopal one. I felt like the timing was right. I wanted to be able to help teens grapple with the cosmic questions of life: Is there a God? What does that have to do with me? Is there a purpose for my life? Questions like that. I couldn't do that in a public-school setting. So, my sense of adventure won out, I was offered the job, and in 2000 I moved to the U.S. By then, ministry was certainly a calling for me. One way or another, I knew I would use my gifts for God's glory all my days.

Bryan: Was it something you even envisioned for yourself and if not, how did you erase the self-doubt that the calling put on you?

Cuyler: When I was younger, I had no interest in following in my father's footsteps. My father is the seventh generation in a row of clergy, seven generations! That's quite a winning streak. To his credit, he never put any pressure on me to keep the ball rolling. In fact, he'd sometimes say the opposite: "Cuy, if there's anything else you can do, do it. Run from the ministry unless and until it hunts you down." In other words, it has to be a calling. And so, I ran from it. For one thing, I never thought I could ever be as good at it as my father. It took years to stop trying to be my father and figure out my own voice and style. But interestingly enough, he had gone through the same thing in learning how to emerge from his own father's shadow.

Bryan: What has been the most impactful part of ministry for you?

Cuyler: I don't mean for this to be a cute answer, but the most impactful part of ministry is when I get out of the way and God does something wonderful through me (or despite me) and I am reminded once again that there is no explanation other than God for the spiritual breakthrough, or the healing, or the life change that occurs in the person I'm serving. It is a high – and a privilege – like no other to be a vessel of grace and/or truth on behalf of the living, dynamic Spirit of God.

Bryan: You and I get along really well and that is partially because of our senses of humor (and striking good looks). You always bring levity, but also take being a pastor very seriously. How do you navigate the challenges of that?

Cuyler: [Writer/theologian] C.S. Lewis declared that "Joy is the serious business of heaven." God is supremely a God of joy. And we are made in his image. A sense of humor – a positive, healthy one – flows out of the deep well of joy that ought to indwell every Christian. Christ-followers have more reason to be joyful than any other people on Earth, and Jesus was the most joy-filled person who ever lived. His mission was deadly serious, but he could not have drawn the outcasts to him the way he did without a joyous spirit, full of hope and compassion. The Pharisees ridiculed him many times for not taking things seriously enough (in their view), which is a badge of honor. Jesus spent as much time telling the religious types to "lighten up" as almost anything else he did.

You can't be a good pastor and not have a sense of humor. You can be a pastor but not a good one, and certainly you won't reflect the playful, lighthearted Jesus who told parables about camels threading needles, and people walking around with two-by-fours in their eyes. A positive, healthy sense of humor is life-giving. If you were stuck on a remote island with either an atheist with a sense of humor or a Christian without a sense of humor, who would you choose? Give me that atheist any day. Lightheartedness is that important for getting through life and helping others get through, too. But ultimately that lightheartedness, to be sustained, must come from a deeper, more profound state – joy. Joy is a fruit of the Spirit – and that makes it a serious gift from God.

Bryan: What do you think is the main misconception about Christians today and how do you combat those who speak out against Christianity?

Cuyler: One main misconception these days is that Christians, in America at least, are predominantly judgmental, narrow-minded, and in lockstep with the Republican Party. There certainly are those, to be sure, but I think the majority of Jesus' disciples in this country are thoughtful, compassionate, humble believers who recognize that they are citizens first of a kingdom far greater than any earthly government, political party, or movement vying for authority. Jesus said, "My kingdom is not of this world" (John 18:36). That ought to be the kingdom we seek first as well. When we do that, we actually make this world a better place in the process. That is the Gospel.

I relate to what the Christian writer Philip Yancey once said. He confessed that when he is in a room full of liberals, he feels like a conservative; and when he is in a room full of conservatives, he feels like a liberal. I think that's a sane place to be in general.

As for those who speak out against Christianity, let them. Some have good points. The historical record of the Church is not without much that is shameful, heartbreaking, and embarrassing to the name of Jesus. But the positive contribution of committed Christians, individually and as a movement of the Body, has been a powerful and overwhelmingly beneficial influence on humanity's story. Christians need to be familiar with that legacy over the centuries, so it can be shared with skeptics. Not in a combative, argumentative way, because that never wins hearts, but in a gracious, good-natured, loving way. Christians who are put on the defensive never need to react defensively. No need to panic over sharing a more honest appraisal of Christianity's mark on this world. When you engage in discussion on the topic with composure, grace, and an utter lack of a need to "win", then you're more likely to earn the right to continue engaging with someone on the subject. The medium is the message after all. And you are the medium, the representative, the conduit, the ambassador, for Christ and his message.

Bryan: I have the privilege of serving beside you at Liquid and have learned a great deal from you. How challenging is it to adapt your mentoring to the different personalities who look to you for guidance?

Cuyler: I don't know that I've ever been conscious of it as a challenge. The important thing is to meet each person at the place and condition they're at in life and go from there. There are single guys in their 20s looking for mentors, as well as middle-aged husbands with three kids. Some are on fire for the Lord and some only know him by word of mouth. Some guys' lives are just beginning, and some are falling apart. The key as a mentor is to pray for wisdom and discernment to know how best to lead each person in their uniqueness. What is their personality? Are they a reader, or not? Visual or aural learner? Introvert or extrovert? Heavy emotional baggage or not much at all? And so on. As a mentor, when you approach the responsibility with humility and ask God to guide you, He'll create pathways for you to lead each person.

Bryan: How has being a husband impacted your pastoring to people and vice versa?

Cuyler: It's certainly given me credibility to walk alongside men, or couples, going through marriage issues, not to mention it's provided me with plenty of material for crafting wedding messages. I've failed countless times in my marriage, but the more I try to fathom the depths of Ephesians 5:25: "A husband should love his wife as much as Christ loved the church and gave his life for it," the more I realize how far I have to go to even scratch the surface of sacrificial living, in terms of my relationship with my wife and my commitment to Jesus' church.

Bryan: If there was one time in your life that you could go back and change on your walk with God, what would it be?

Cuyler: That's easy. I would have surrendered to Him earlier. I made a lot of relationship mistakes, hurt people, in my late teens and early 20s that could have been avoided if I'd been listening to God.

Bryan: What advice do you give to people who have a hunger in their hearts to serve God and how do you bring people to that realization to the surface if they don't see it in themselves?

Cuyler: I used to have a poster on my office door when I was a youth pastor. It said: "Love God, love people. The rest is details." That's the Gospel in a nutshell. You want to serve God? Serve people. Talk to God, talk to people. Be humble before God, be humble before people. Put God first, then everything else. It's the acronym for JOY: Jesus-Others-You. That's the order. Life gets out of whack when that's not the order. Everyone has a hunger for God. The problem is that many chase a false god (power, career, sex, financial security, fame) thinking it will satisfy the hunger. It may for a while, but never for long. If someone tells me they don't hunger for God, I might say, "Tell me about what you do hunger for (i.e., your desires, hopes and dreams), and then maybe we can talk about somebody who promises to fill you to the brim with a life that takes away the deepest thirsts and hungers, and I have to be prepared to share my own experience of life-change.

Bryan: Besides great hair, one of your other giftings is being a cartoonist with a religious slant to the cards, etc. What (pardon the pun) drew you to that?

Cuyler: I've been drawing ever since I could hold a Crayola. In 2003 I started a line of greeting cards and other products called *Inherit the Mirth*. It's often described as "*The Far Side* meets the Bible." If you don't know Gary Larson's cartoons, look them up. You can also look up mine at www.cuylerblack.com. There are hundreds. I hope you like them. I guess you could say my vision statement for my little company is Genesis 21:6: "God has brought me laughter." I want to be counted among the Christians who bring light and laughter and joy to people.

Bryan: Being a pastor is often labor intensive both physically and mentally. How do you find balance in your life?

Cuyler: Although I don't succeed anywhere near as often as I'd like to, for me the key is to be disciplined with the right priorities of God first, my wife second, my son third, and then everyone else. I need to be a priority, too, somewhere in there, or else I won't be any good to anyone else. So, physical fitness is important, eating right, and finding time for the activities that bring me personal pleasure, like writing, reading, hiking.

My father, the pastor, used to say, "The church is a jealous mistress." Healthy boundaries are vital to serving with excellence your family, the church, and yourself over the long haul. Invite others you trust to meet with you and speak into your life. A healthy pastor is proactive about having a mentor, a counselor, a trusted friend, beyond just one's spouse, to lean into, and to be held accountable by, in the most grace-filled and truth-filled ways possible.

Cuyler is the Spiritual Care Pastor and the Groups Pastor at Liquid Church. He came on staff in May 2012. He and wife, Lisa, have one son, Xander. Cuyler is also a talented cartoonist who has a series of greeting cards, Inherit The Mirth. For more information visit: www.cuylerblack.com/.

Adam Ellenberger

Bryan: Did your walk with God start at an early age?

Adam: My grandfather was a pastor, as was his father. A lot of my uncles are pastors. Church is very much a part of our family, and my upbringing was predominantly Christian and Missionary Alliance. I grew up going to Sunday school and the music at the time was predominantly hymns. My parents loved them because they grew up with them, so that was what I was introduced to.

I was able to say "The Lord's Prayer" when I was four. It meant something to me even at that age. I knew my parents were happy and it was something that I wanted to do, but they let me do that in my own time. I have rediscovered what that meant throughout the years and recommitted myself several times since, at important times in my life.

Bryan: Did you go through times when you rebelled against being close to God?

Adam: Your walk with God changes. As you mature, you learn new things about yourself and what it means to be a Christian, what it means to be dedicated to a supernatural power that governs the universe. My walk has been something that I do not just take at face value, because I was very cognizant that this is something my parents believed in.

I did not necessarily go through rebellious phases, but I definitely went through times of doubt, questioning and just needing to validate for myself what I believed. I wanted to make sure that I was overcoming any kind of perception that my parents would have potentially placed on me.

Bryan: Was it during high school?

Adam: I think seventh grade was a pivotal year for me. I was going through a lot during that time and I was probably going through one of my hardest years of depression. I struggled with depression a lot in my teenage years and even younger. It was around that time that that was a very interpersonal thing, where I stripped away what existence meant. I wanted to understand what was at the core of things and what truth was. Fortunately, in my darkest of times, even when I was young, the thing that I came to is that God is real and that loving Him is probably one of the biggest callings a human can have.

On that foundation, I was able to overcome times where doubt would creep in and I experienced difficulties in my walk, in my late teen years, even into college. I would always come back to that same thing I discovered at the beginning when I was young.

That is a message that has lasted throughout the years for me. The simplicity of the message of the gospel and that you, a human with a psyche, can waiver to and from. But you know at your core that your relationship with God and His direct involvement in your life is a very real thing. It takes two to cultivate that relationship. That foundation is why I am the way I am today.

Bryan: I have also suffered from depression and it was hard during that time to lean on God because your mind is playing tricks on you. Did you have a similar or different experience?

Adam: Absolutely. I would find myself, like you mentioned, crippled almost. I was unable to even just take physical action. I think when I was young, I was trying to reconcile what that actually meant. I found that was a flaw within myself at the time and turned that into self-loathing.

Your emotions are a rollercoaster when you are going through depression. There are ups and down. But what I found at the time and what has even helped me cope with depression now, was the foundation in God that my parents laid out for me.

To be honest, it was around seventh grade that I was suicidal. I knew that it would be wrong for me to do it, but there was still something that was pulling me toward it. Once I was looking at my emotions as subjective, something that is going to come and go, that informed me for the rest of my life. Now when I come to darker times in my life, even now, I recognize the existence of this thing that is happening to me outside of my control.

Bryan: Going through depression there is a lot of "feelings are not facts". But when you're mired down in that depression, self-doubt and self-loathing, it is hard to see that. I very much relate to everything you are saying.

Adam: It is interesting when you bring it up, how many people can relate. But everybody has their own journey and they find their own way out of it.

For me, God is so omnipresent. Maybe this is part of something that I need to overcome as well, but I didn't allow that thought to occur that God is there no matter what. God is there through the good times and the bad times. I always never wanted to be one of those people who needed God only when I needed Him.
I want to need him at my happiest and at my darkest. Coming through the depression informed me and made me even more grateful for the life I was given. It also gave me compassion for others and the life they were given and also to treat life as sacred.

I think that the positive thing that came from all of that, especially with my spiritual growth, is you can say that you only live once, and you want to do a lot of things in this life.

But so much of that actually also applies to your faith. Every single day you have the opportunity to experience something new or something interesting. But you also have the opportunity to pray, to show love and compassion to somebody, where maybe you couldn't have before.

I have always felt like love and life was precious. But I think coming through that in my younger years made me doubly determined to live a life that was worthy of the kingdom. That was my takeaway.

Bryan: Who on this side of Heaven helped you get through it?

Adam: I had a really great youth group fortunately, in high school. I know a lot of kids didn't have that. There were friends that I had made that were secular friends, and one of my best friends ended up coming to my church and we were able to go through high school together, going through this same youth group.

I was somebody who had walked on the fence for a while in terms of friendships. I got along with everybody. I wasn't the in-your-face Christian kid. I think that I had a lot of worry in my younger years about that. Sometimes I felt like I was not doing enough for God, not inviting kids to church, etc.

I learned just from being a follower of Christ, how much respect that garnered from my friends. I began to notice and understand that I was the guy that people would come to. It was not just coming to me to talk something out. They came to me when it came to deep questions, intense conversation or even the emotions that people are uncomfortable with, like existence or death. I tend to be the person in my family and with my friends that they could talk to.

Even friends that weren't saved, I found out that I was their moral standard in secular terms, of what a good person is.

Bryan: Did that surprise you?

Adam: Yeah. In a lot of ways. I guess my qualm with the world is that I think people should be decent to each other. I've been fortunate enough to have been given the tools to actually live that life. It always amazes me how much people appreciate that is my baseline.

I think that has largely to do with my family, my father's example and what was imbued in me as a kid. I found that I was able to have an impact on people spiritually through being there for them and being somebody who's going to have that deep conversation with them, somebody who is going to lend that advice when it's needed.

I worked that out with God. I always wanted to be the person who would lead the legions to Christ. But I think that my gift is in the small things, in ministering to people on a very personal level in one-on-one conversations.

When I was younger, I would be very subversive about it. People brought up conversations around the questions of, "Do I hook up with this girl? Do I do this or that?" at very young ages. I would actually be ministering to them without them knowing it. Kind of like, "Well, let's think about the pros and cons of this. What's this going to do? What doors is this going to open?" My secular friends were able to understand over time that it was God's influence in me that I was sharing with them.

I can tell a phony a mile away. I can't abide plastic, phony platitudes and blanket advice that sounds good. I need to feel that somebody cares, if I'm going to listen to their advice. I need to feel that what I'm being given is authentic. And I think that's what I'm able to give to other people.

Bryan: How many people do you think that you've mentored throughout the years?

Adam: I've had a few people tell me how much certain instances meant to them and how influential or impactful a certain conversation or a certain concept was that was introduced to them, which for me, was everything. That is validation I wasn't expecting, but it was an awesome gift that I was being handed.

When you really want to live life to its fullest or there's a depth to that, that allows you not to want to waste words with people. I go through life thinking that every moment could potentially have a meaning to it.

Bryan: You serve on Liquid Worship playing the electric guitar and have also been part of different bands. Where did your interest in music start?

Adam: I guess my introduction was Nirvana and Green Day and learning those types of songs that were all power chords. I also liked Jimi Hendrix and my brother would bring home music like DC Talk and bands like that. I liked that they were Christian, but there was just something about the tone of some worship music that didn't pull me in. I am like a magnet to more intense music. I like heavy music, but I also like really ambient music. I like everything. It's like for me a good song is a good song.

I was like that when I was really young. My parents said I would hear song on radio and want to hear it over and over, whether it be a pop song or Mozart. There is something in a song to me that's ephemeral, that pulls me in. And if a song has that quality, doesn't matter what the genre is, I like it. But I will say most of the time it's evocative and perhaps on the darker side. I still love my dance music, for the floor. I like everything, but it's got to have something.

I taught myself to play guitar. In the beginning I picked up a guitar and I wasn't playing anything that made any sense, but I was feeling what I was playing. And I was like, "This is me. This is the future. I'm going to become a guitarist."

I must have been around 13 and me and my neighbors started a band. I got my neighbor to play bass and the kid up the road to play drums. That was when I started being in bands and oftentimes, I was in two bands at the same time.

There would always be one with anybody who wanted to get together and jam and then another band at church that I was playing in. In high school, I convinced some of the guys in youth group to start playing punk. We wrote an EP and I sent it to Tooth & Nail Records and never heard anything back. That was my first recorded effort, I guess you could say.

Around that time, Christian music was changing. My church finally got a drum set and they had one service with hymns and another service with instruments. They asked if the youth group would like to play. We would play Saturday nights every now and then where we would just jam out on our stuff. Then we had one night where my Christian youth group pop punk band played at our church.

One time a woman who organized an event we were at did not appreciate our music. I turned on my distorted guitar and started doing my thing, she covered her ears and said, "You can't do that." And I said, "What do you mean?" She's like, "That sounds like broken glass. And I do not want you to play that here." I turned it down and turned off my gain [sound effect for guitars] and I was really crestfallen after that. That was kind of like the end of that chapter before I left for college. There was an explosion of new music coming out at that time. I started with new stuff that I found interesting.

After I graduated college, I continued to play in bands. I became friends with someone who would later become a drummer. I was in my mid-20s at this point and we started a band that we were trying to take really seriously.

We started playing a lot of local shows and playing anything that we could. We weren't a Christian band. It was like a metal hardcore band. I was writing most of the music and I had a huge influence on the lyrics, but the vocalist wasn't really all about my message. So, it would get twisted here and there. There was a bit of a conflict, but we were still able to do what we wanted to do. We did that for a little while and tried to play as many shows as we could.

We ended up merging with another band in 2012. We started a new band and we got another vocalist, so we had a singer and a screamer named Christian.

We laid down tracks and made a demo. But in Christian, I found a brother in Christ. At this point we were both going to be writing the lyrics for this new project. The rest of the band wasn't saved and at the time there was so much going on that was very counterculture and what was being released was very provocative.

The band ended up being signed to an indie label. And we ended up touring. I left a lucrative job to try and be a professional musician.

There were great Christian bands coming out at the time who were actually doing fantastic. But then there was also backlash in that, where a lot of those bands have said that they're no longer Christian today, which is unfortunate.

Bryan: That was a huge leap of faith.

Adam: It was, but being a musician was so central to what I felt has always been my mission in life.

It was about two years into that endeavor where my label and our manager wanted us to make a music video that was really provocative and would kind of shock everybody. The band members looked at me and I was like, "Well, I guess you have to break it to him that this isn't what we are about." That was the beginning of the end for me, where God was tugging at my heart.

That was another one of those breakthrough moments for me in my walk, where I said, "God, this is killing me that my dream is going to die. You're asking me to let my dream die. But I need to take that in faith."

I had the meeting and I kind of went my separate way while still supporting this band, because they were going to still go on tour. I was going to still write with them, but it was kind of the end for me.

There were bands at the time that were just really putting out content that was raw and real about their experience with God and their faith. It was very inspiring to me.

There are songs that I have written that nobody knows, that are kind of like prayers to God. Even just sitting, playing the guitar and having a moment where you're fully immersed and just grateful that God put you on the planet. You can have this experience with your instrument and these tones that are washing over you. To me, that's worship as well.

Bryan: That's rough.

Adam: It was really rough. It felt like a part of me had died because I let my dream go. A week or two after that, I was finding myself in a depression. I went to a service at Liquid and sat in the back. During that service the worship leader put out a call for anyone who was a musician to try out. It was like God shone a light on me right onto my heart. The tug I felt was palpable. I tried out and the rest is history, and that was about seven years ago.

Bryan: What advice would you give to someone looking for a career in the music industry?

Adam: I definitely think people should follow their dreams. If you love music, don't let anything get in the way. At the same time, be a realist about what the environment's like out there. You're not going to be handed everything. Whatever dream you have in your head, you kind of need to put that aside to look at the reality of things.

If you are in it for the wrong reasons, that is a tell-tale sign that music is great, but it is also something that can be used for bad. It is something that could be used as a litmus test for where culture's going.

Music influences communication between people. We can become desensitized to ideas and we can also be enlightened. It is up to you to have the responsibility to make something that is either putting positivity out to the world or it could be a destructive force.

Bryan: It is hard to not get wrapped up during the worship part of Sunday services, whether on stage or in the seats. It is great seeing the musicians and vocalists having their own personal moments of revelation while also doing that for those of us who are watching.

Adam: I have gotten feedback on this worship team that I tend to be one of those people who gets into it. That is something that just happens to me and something that I give into, because that is literally the reason that I love music. First and foremost, we want to minister and open up the way to the kingdom for the people who are there. But for me, God speaks to me while I am playing. It is just so amazing. When you know you are prepared, know your parts and you are just dialed into the energy in the room, it is incredible.

Even right down to the way you are playing your instrument or singing, it is all in praise. Worshipping God isn't just the lyrics. It's every hit of every drum, every strum of every guitar. I am somebody who values those moments more than anything.

Bryan: What were some of your biggest moments on your walk with God?

Adam: I was baptized by the youth pastor at the church that I grew up in when I was 15 or 16, alongside one of my best friends. It was a really important moment.

My parents were there, and I articulated at the time exactly what I was hoping to say, which was, "I know that I'll fall down and I'll get up and I'll fall down and I'll get up. And I just look forward to the day that I'll fall up and wake up in eternity."

The baptism itself was a very moving experience, to the point where I thought often about doing it again. I'm sure I will someday, but that was my baptism as far as I'm concerned.

Bryan: You are married and have a daughter, with another baby on the way. How important was it for you when you were single to find someone who shared the same Christian values that you did?

Adam: It was essential. I had gone through relationships in high school and I had gone through some heartache that left me rather jaded. But in the end I still have to give praise to my parents for the amazing example they set for me. I had a set of criteria that I was steadfast on that I would never waiver from.

I knew that my wife would be Christian, that we would raise a Christian family, that we would have to have very similar values in terms of our morality and really out of the heart of love comes trust.

I knew that I had to implicitly trust somebody in order to marry them. I relied on God to bring me that person and it took a long time. I married way later in my life and that's because I had made a commitment. I had said, "I'm willing to die alone unless the right person comes along." I was not going to marry just for the sake of marrying. I'm not going to treat this with any kind of frivolity.

Bryan: That's so counter-cultural to what people think now.

Adam: Yes. My parents raised me to be counterculture and they instilled in me that type of value. While I saw friends around me and other people just doing the opposite, that was something so core to me that I just knew that it was just going to happen someday. If for some reason it didn't, I had already made peace with that.

My wife and I ended up dating for quite a long time. God had some refining to do. There was trust that needed to be established and maintained over a period of time. That wasn't all me and my wife totally agrees with that.

I was very vocal throughout that time about what I wanted, and we talked through where we needed to be to get married. We kept that line of communication open.
.

We talked about it a lot and we would be very honest about ourselves about how far we were away from that at times. We eventually just had a mountaintop moment and it brought everything to a head. It wasn't a good mountaintop moment. It was actually like a trench in the mountain, because we were literally talking about ending it. Then it came together so beautifully, and God really spoke to us in the moment. He made me realize that this is the person I'm spending the rest of my life with.

It's almost like how some people need to see the darkness before they have their breakthrough. That was kind of the moment that we had. It was beautiful. In His timing, He put on our hearts to get married. I honestly didn't propose, we just all of a sudden said, "It's time to get married." As a joke, the day before our actual wedding that was planned, I brought her out to a lake in Colorado and proposed to her.

Bryan: You mentioned your strong relationship you have with your parents. Are you raising your daughter and soon to arrive second child in the same way you were raised?

Adam: I think having parents that have the moral integrity to practice what they preach, to be there for their kids and to make family the priority, is the greatest gift that you can give a child and I am immensely grateful for that gift from my parents.

I want to do the same thing with my children. I want to be there for them. My parents come from an older generation that was definitely more authoritarian. I think that for my children, I am not trying to be their best friend, but I certainly want them to be able to speak to me about anything without fear. I want them to always feel that Dad is going to have a word for them that matters and to never be afraid to share the good and the bad with me.

I am going to do everything I can to earn that. I want to prove to my kids that I will nourish them, and I'll treat anything that they bring to me with respect and I won't laugh it off. I will apply the empathy that I naturally have into my child rearing, but I'm very cognizant of what the world's going to be throwing at them. I intend to be very involved and to always have the conversation going and never let it fall off.

Adam is a guitarist on the Liquid Worship team. In his professional life, he is a full-time scientist. In his personal life, he pursues many walks as a music producer, outdoor enthusiast, investor and "perpetual student of life." Adam's faith began early in his life through active Bible-based parenting, but it was his personal confrontation with depression and his relentless search for truth that matured his faith to make him an advocate for mental health, honest self-assessment, empathy and personal well-being.

Bryan: Did you grow up as a churchgoer and if so, what was your denomination?

Derek: I grew up in a Pentecostal Assemblies of God church here in New Jersey. And yes, major churchgoer. I went every week. My parents brought me to Bible study, prayer meetings, choir, and worship team rehearsals. It was non-stop.

Bryan: What are your early memories/impressions of church?

Derek: My early memories are always of the typical Black Pentecostal church. Vibrant, fiery, expressive, high-energy worship. Lots of shouting, music and people dancing almost every Sunday. Preaching was very spirit-led, never series-based or planned out ahead of time. My earliest memories were of me sitting in church, drawing pictures on the bulletins, and trying to be as quiet as possible during sermons. I was always told to be super-respectful in church, and that the church leaders were the spiritual authorities and deserved to be listened to.

Bryan: When did you discover your vocal ability, and was it because of being part of a worship team/church choir?

Derek: I've always been a part of the worship/music ministry at pretty much every church I've been a part of. I honestly don't know when I discovered my vocal ability. I kind of stumbled on it while singing in choirs or worship teams as a kid/teen. I did go through a number of years where I wouldn't sing in church and only played keys. When I moved to Chicago, I was pushed into more of a worship leader role, which had me singing more.

Bryan: Did you go through any seasons of your life where your faith was tested?

Derek: I feel like faith tests are a constant part of life. I'm constantly wondering about where my faith is. I think one of the hardest times of my life faith-wise was when I first moved to Chicago. I was in a new city, alone, no family around and trying to find my way in life without any real support. I found a church home, but hadn't made a community yet. I found myself spiraling negatively and not seeking God for guidance in that season. There's truth to the thought that "isolation is dangerous", and that isolation includes separation from God. You start to try to fill the void left from that relationship with things that are "ungodly". It's really a vicious cycle.

Bryan: What led you back to Him?

Derek: Honestly, it was the realization of what I was doing to fill the gap apart from God. I was looking at myself more critically asking, "What am I doing?" Through that God spoke to me and drew me back.

Bryan: You have been part of, or led, different worship teams and are now the Worship Leader at Liquid's Mercer County location. What experiences shaped who you are within the church?

Derek: I feel like I have a really unique perspective on the lowercase 'c' church. I've been built up and torn down by people in the church. I've been told I was 'loved' and then completely forgotten about when I left churches. I had developed some of (what I thought) were some of my best relationships and friendships through the church only to now never really hear from those same people.

So, for me, those experiences with church people shaped who I am within the church. I tend to shy away from deeper relationships because I take relationships very seriously and seek to go deep with them, which leaves you more vulnerable to hurts. I find myself cringing at certain phrases and sayings that the church usually says, especially when "love" is used.

Now, I say all this while being a worship leader. I still believe in the church community. I believe that there's value in it. I think for me, it'll take time to work through some of the recent hurts from the church community. I'm thankful for Liquid's community in that there's a different air about it overall. It doesn't reduce my caution, but the way it's done at Liquid allows me to feel a level of comfort.

Bryan: Who were some of your mentors?

Derek: Definitely my mom and dad. I've had worship leaders from various churches mentor me with worship. But the most mentorship is from my parents. They've guided me through so many aspects of my young adult and adult life.

Bryan: It is inevitable to be let down by your Christian brothers and sisters at some point. Without naming someone specifically, can you give an example of a relationship that you thought was one thing and ended up being another?

Derek: Like I mentioned before, I've built really strong friendships within small groups, and within church communities that I thought were lifelong. By my standards, a friend, a good friend, is there when you're at your lowest. What I realized is that a lot of friendships now are situational or based on proximity. Once a variable changes, the relationship changes, which frustrates me.

But, again, I'm learning to adjust my lens around relationships and the who's who in my life from those experiences. No matter how the relationship started, I won't allow myself to invest to the level where I could be hurt. There's only a small, like two, relationships I have in my life to that depth.

Bryan: What is your leadership style?

Derek: I like to lead from a place of collaboration. I want teams I lead to feel like I'm in the trenches with them as opposed to pushing them in without me. I want individuals on my team to thrive in their giftings and be their best selves in whatever role, whether ministry or secular.

Additionally, I like teams to feel comfortable. Comfortable to tell me no without worry of being guilted. Comfortable to ask questions or challenge my ideas. Comfortable to give their ideas. Comfortable to be who God made them to be and become an all-star in their role.

Bryan: You have a commanding presence on stage leading your congregation to God. I know you take it very seriously. What stressors come along with that?

Derek: The biggest stressor with being on a platform is not allowing the response of the people to get to my head or become about me. It's a battle to stay grounded there to be honest, especially when on a platform like the one at the Parsippany campus. Every time I'm on a platform, I'm actively reminding myself that it's not about me.

Bryan: What has been the greatest season of your life and why?

Derek: 2021. That year was incredible. Me and my family were fresh off moving back to NJ from Texas after a really hard season of culture shock and loss after we left the church we were a part of there. 2020 was just a hard year, not only losing a church family, but Covid struck, and we were isolated in a state that was just hostile for us as an interracial family. The racism runs so deep there you could almost taste it in the air.

Coming back to NJ, the familiarity, our families, our friendships here, was incredible in and of itself. Add the fact that I was thriving at Liquid, my wife was back to teaching at her old school of 11 years and the kids were now able to grow up around their family.

On top of that, God opened a door for us to buy a great home around the corner from where my wife taught and the kids attended, in a market where homes were being purchased for $50,000 to 60,000 over asking price and *under* the appraised amount. Not only that, but I also landed a dream project management job through a person who worked at Liquid. It was because of a conversation I had with her on her last day at Liquid, before moving out of state. It was just a wild year of positives.

Bryan: How have you navigated racism in your life, whether it came from people where you were serving, or in everyday life?

Derek: I've come to realize that racism, like any other "ism", is a byproduct of a person's surroundings and perspective. I believe there are three things that make a person who they are: 1) You're the average of the five people you're around the most 2) You're a product of your environment 3) You're the sum total of your life experiences. If these three factors have a limited view of someone different than you or have been influenced by someone who has a negative view of a people group, then naturally racism follows.

With all that being said, my view on racism is much different at 40 than it was at 20. When I was younger, I was pulled over several times for "fitting the description" by police. I have been searched by officers who had their hands on their guns. I have been told as recently as three years ago that I was "big and scary" or "dressed like a drug dealer". I've been held back from jobs and promotions. I have been tokenized for being Black in a primarily white church under the guise of the "multi-ethnic church", but I was really there to be one of the Black faces used to fly that banner.

So how have I navigated it? I've learned to remember the three things that make people who they are and attempt to broaden people's perspectives by talking openly about the things I've faced or am facing as a Black man. I'm also unapologetically myself *always* -- Jordans, jean jackets and graphic tees. Why? Because for a long time I adjusted who I was to make others comfortable, and it was a detriment to my mental health and well-being. There's no time for that any longer. Lastly, I've learned that what people think of me is none of my business, until they try to harm me or my family in any way because of how they think.

Bryan: How hard do you have to lean in on God to deal with that?

Derek: It took a lot of prayer and self-reflection to get to the place that I am at with racism. I had to realize that we all struggle with some type of brokenness and who am I to judge a person based on that. It's not easy, because I do get angry when I see racial injustices and the trauma that comes with it. I still feel the effects every time there is a story that is released about another shooting or another hashtag. But God has really worked in me to help me to see it for what it is, sin and brokenness.

Bryan: You have a beautiful family and are their protector, as God is all of ours. Did things you learned within a church setting/being influenced by Jesus help get you to that point?

Derek: Yes and no. Obviously the Bible and the direction of the word of God is very explicit in explaining what I should be as a husband and a father, so I take that seriously. But what was modeled for me from my parents and from strong men around me shaped how I am as a father and husband. Now, am I great at it? I wouldn't say that by any means. I struggle and struggle hard. I make mistakes. But life is a journey, and we are all works in process.

Bryan: Being a leader, you have the opportunity to mentor. Is there anyone that you have fulfilled that role for and what has being one brought to your life?

Derek: I honestly don't know. I've worked with so many people, and have been around so many great artists, musicians, and worship leaders, I don't even know who I've officially mentored or played that role for. I just know that whomever I'm around, I want to share what I am and what I know with them. If that helps them grow or learn in any way, whether I know about it or not, it's a win for me.

Derek is the Worship Leader at Liquid Church's Mercer County campus and works as a Senior Project Manager at Thermo Fisher Scientific. He and his wife, Linnea, share two children, Benjamin and Isabella.

Dani Santana

Bryan: Were religion and God a big part of your life from an early age?

Dani: I remember going to church since I was very little. I have been blessed with parents who love God and are prayer warriors, so church was very important in our lives growing up. However, my relationship with God grew when I turned 10. This was also the year I started playing the guitar and drums at church and have been involved in worship teams ever since.

Bryan: What foundations did your family instill in you when it came to spirituality?

Dani: I grew up hearing this constantly in my house: "Love God with all your heart, and with all your strength". We learned from an early age to pray and seek God for anything and everything.

Bryan: Being a teenage/young adult comes with its own challenges. How did you lean in on God to keep you from straying?

Dani: I thank God for using me in worship since an early age, so my high school and college years I was always playing in different Christian bands, touring, conferences, youth camps, Sunday services, etc. So pretty much worship kept me from straying.

Bryan: Did friends give you a hard time or try to distract you from having God as a central figure in your life? Did you lose friendships because of it, whether you distanced yourself from them or them stepping out of your life?

Dani: When I wasn't in church, I was also involved in different types of sports. My friends there also kept me away from getting in trouble. There was always a tournament coming up or training to go to. I was always known as the "Christian kid" so they tried behaving as much as they could when I was around.

Bryan: You are married and have two beautiful daughters. How did you and your wife meet? Was she a devout Christian?

Dani: I met my wife at church. I remember one day I was playing the drums at a youth event and saw her walking into service.

Bryan: What challenges have you faced as a couple that God has pulled you through?

Dani: One of the most difficult times we faced as a couple was with our second pregnancy. The first challenge was that my wife needed surgery to keep our baby safe. Second, she ended up delivering our second daughter at just 29 weeks. We spent the next 49 days living in the NICU, feeling all sorts of emotions during this time: fear, sadness, anger, helplessness but also, hope, trust, and love, lots and lots of love. Some days were really hard. We felt defeated sometimes and did not know what the outcome was going to be, but we also never felt alone. God was there during this difficult time as well; we truly felt that God was in control. Fast-forward to now, we have been blessed with the funniest, healthiest princess. This is why when we sing "Another in the Fire", I get reminded of the many times that we've been through hard times, but He is always there, helping us through.

Bryan: Your daughters are going to be raised by a family of people of faith. Does the way society is headed in terms of "anything goes" worry you in relation to raising your daughters?

Dani: Yes, I worry about how sometimes it is easier and more accepting for someone to go with the flow than to stand up for your principles and beliefs. I can only pray that God gives my wife, Eimy, and I the wisdom that we need to guide our girls to live a life where God is at the center of their lives. We also want to be able to provide a family where they find love, security, and forgiveness. We want to be good examples of fatherly love and what it is to live a Christian life.

Bryan: As a member of the Liquid Worship, how does it feel to be part of a team that brings people closer to God?

Dani: It is a gift from God that I've been a part of since 2010. What a blessing it is for me to be able to worship with some of the best musicians I know. I also know this is a privilege and thank God every time I am on stage and pray that my playing brings someone closer to His presence.

Bryan: If you were to give advice to a young Christian male today, what would it be?

Dani: Surround yourself with people that love God. I would say to also trust that God is in control, even if it does not make sense at the moment. God has a plan in your life, and He will come through as promised.

Dani plays drums on the Liquid Worship team and serves as the senior accountant at Liquid Church. He and his wife, Eimy, have two daughters, Emilia and Sofia.

Dave Brooks

Bryan: How important was God/church in your formative years?

Dave: I was really blessed to have been raised in a Christian home. My story begins with my grandparents who served God as missionaries in the Philippines and endured incredible hardships during WWII. My father was born there and after coming back to the US and settling down to raise a family, my parents obeyed God's calling on their lives and they also served in the Philippines. I sailed across the Pacific at age 4 and most of my years prior to graduating high school were spent in the Philippines.

I really enjoyed my years as a "missionary kid". In addition to all the adventure as a young boy, as I grew older, I also formed lifelong friendships. My siblings and I attended an excellent international school that was started for Christian kids in the Far East. It grew to be a large K-12 school where I was taught rigorous academics, played competitive athletics, and had Christian men and women who didn't just teach me at school but modeled for me what it meant to be a follower of Jesus Christ. Although, I trusted Jesus as a 7-year-old, and during my high school years I got serious about my faith.

Bryan: Were there times in your life that you questioned what God was doing in it?

Dave: There have been plenty of times in my life, because of disappointments and losses that I didn't understand what I should be doing or what the next step was, but I really haven't struggled with questioning God. Most times when I have stopped to compare the hard experiences with how very fortunate I've been, I have realized how thankful I am for God's goodness instead of questioning His sovereignty.

Despite being at an outstanding Christian school, Wheaton College, I struggled to adjust. For one thing, can you imagine how cold I was? Going from the heat of the Philippines to the frigid temperatures in the "Windy City" of Chicago was a huge shock to my system! Those years were significantly harder than any I'd previously experienced. The biggest challenge I had and often still do, is feeling that God loves me. While I have always known the truth that God loves me, I haven't always felt that He did. I've struggled with believing that He could love a selfish, stoic, average person like me.

I'm incredibly grateful that God has provided countless situations where I read just the right verse or passage from the Bible that I needed to hear. God has also sent numerous people, primarily my wife, Lois, who have shown their love for me as an example of Christ's love. One specific example happened years ago when a counselor kindly made me aware that I didn't feel that God loved me. He wrote on a sheet of paper the following statements, "There is nothing I can do to earn more of God's love, He loves me just the way I am. There is nothing I can do to lose any of God's love. He loves me just the way I am." I kept that piece of paper in my pocket for several years, reading it daily to help me solidify the truth in my heart and not just in my mind that God loves me.

Bryan: When did you decide to fulfill your calling to become a pastor?

Dave: My story of becoming a pastor was more because of God's provision than my decision. I was the US chief financial officer (CFO) of a global industrial gas company that was acquired in September, 2006. At that point, I thought I would be out of a job since they didn't need two US CFOs. My wife and I went away for an anniversary weekend later that month and were talking and praying about what I was going to do next in my career.

I had been giving some business help at Liquid Church as the first conversations began about launching out as a separate church in 2007. I told her that if there was a job at Liquid, I would consider taking it. The day after we got back, I was approached by Liquid leadership saying, "We have to figure out a way to get you to come work for Liquid." Over the next two months, God confirmed in several distinct ways that He was calling me to join the team as the executive pastor.

For example, at the end of the two-month period, the finance director of the acquiring company came over from Germany to meet with me. I anticipated the meeting was to discuss transition and timing, but instead he offered me the job as the CFO of the combined companies in the US. I thanked him for the offer but let him know that I'd already decided to go work for my church. He couldn't quite understand, so he came back with an increased compensation offer two weeks later.

When I went home the night of the offer Lois and I talked and prayed. We were at complete peace about our decision to partner with God in the work of growing Liquid. In retrospect, I have seen this as a wonderful confirming gift that God gave me. It wasn't that I was backing into ministry because I was out of a job, but I knew for certain that God had opened the door and wanted to use me at Liquid.

Bryan: You currently serve as Executive Pastor at Liquid Church, where I have the absolute privilege of being a volunteer staff member. Liquid has three core tenets - Grace Wins; Truth is Relevant; Church is Fun. Why did you land on those three specifically?

Dave: From the beginning of Liquid, we have always valued the wonderful counterbalance of grace and truth as evidenced by Jesus and communicated in the Bible. A key verse related to our values is John 1:14, "We have seen His glory, the glory of the one and only Son, who came from the Father, full of grace and truth." Jesus modeled being full of grace and truth, but it's significant to note that He led with grace during His days on Earth. So, based on Christ's example, we see these as core biblical values that Grace Wins and Truth is Relevant.

We also believe that church should be refreshing. We want people who walk through our doors to not just come to learn and worship, but also to enjoy being in a community. While there could be other ways to say this, we believe "Church is fun" helps us remember to include those attractional, enriching, and enjoyable moments in what we do at Liquid.

Bryan: One of my favorite things about Liquid is that you subscribe to "faith is a journey, not a guilt trip," which is such an important statement when it comes to our walk with God. Do you think that has led to the success and growth at Liquid Church?

Dave: Our vision is to "Saturate the State with the gospel of Jesus Christ." We want everyone in New Jersey, as well as throughout the world, to experience the good news of the gospel, which is that everyone can have a relationship with Jesus. I don't want people to join a religion, or follow a set of religious codes or beliefs, but along with the rest of the leadership team, we want them to follow Jesus and have a loving, intimate, enriching relationship with Him. This is a process or a journey of taking steps that can look different for each of us. Continuing to walk in the direction of loving Him and knowing the joy of an ongoing relationship is the lifelong pursuit of every Christ follower. There should be no guilt or shame about where each of us are on that pathway. Instead of evaluating where others are or feeling guilt, I pray that each one of us continues to embrace the journey that Jesus has envisioned for us.

Bryan: You have a beautiful family. What did you and Lois instill in Meg, Robby, and Kate growing up, and even still to this day?

Dave: Every day I thank God for the incredible blessing of three beautiful children, two wonderful sons-in-law, and now four adorable grandchildren! Each one of them are priceless gifts from God…beautiful, precious, and completely undeserved gifts! Candidly, I believe I've learned more from them than they have from me. I often fall short of what I want to be as a dad and for sure we are not a "Hallmark family" where all we do is marvelous and an example to be followed by others.

But I have made it my priority to make sure that each of them knows they are deeply loved. Although we have often fallen short…and continue to, we spend time encouraging them, supporting them, helping them see how special they are, and letting them know they are deeply loved by us and most importantly by God. Undeniably, both Lois and I know that our daily prayers for their specific needs have made a difference. It may sound simplistic, but it is God's amazing grace to us, and not what we've done, that has been the reason for a family although not perfect, brings us such *joy*.

Bryan: Your son, Robby, is part of the special needs community, which Liquid Church passionately supports and is so inclusive of. As a pastor and a father, how does it make you feel to see Robby thrive at Liquid?

Dave: Your use of the word thrive is spot on because that is exactly what Robby does at Liquid. His favorite days of the week are the ones he comes to serve at Liquid, now in the café and previously as a volunteer in a variety of other roles. He has formed wonderful relationships and been encouraged to not just be present but to grow. We joke and call Robby the Mayor, since more people seem to know him than me. I love to be known as "Robby's dad" instead of Pastor Dave!

Lois and I are so deeply grateful for the Special Needs leadership at Liquid that has created a culture of inclusion and an environment where Robby and his peers are welcomed, accepted, and seen as uniquely created and loved by God and many others in our church.

Our desire for our son was that he'd be taught about Jesus and His love, not just at home but by other committed Christ followers in a church. When we thought of our baby boy's spiritual future it seemed very unlikely that we would experience our desires for him.

Now 35 years later, we've seen our specific prayers for him be answered above and beyond what we imagined. It reminds me to not limit God with my own ideas or doubts, but to make my requests known and then watch Him show up. Even if I wrote notes all day for a week, I'm pretty sure that we still wouldn't be able to thank all the amazing people we've known at Liquid who have loved our son so well. I am forever grateful!

Bryan: You have been a mentor to many, many people throughout the years, some you may not have even known about. How does it feel to be seen as such a strong man of faith, a family man and one of the kindest people that God has entrusted to lead the staff?

Dave: I'm humbled and appreciate your kind words, but I don't really see myself that way. What I do know is that I am very committed to doing whatever I can to help the people who work with me to grow and mature in their roles professionally and most importantly in their journey with Jesus. I truly want to see the staff I work with, and am deeply committed to shepherding, realize their God-given potential and His plans for their lives.

Bryan: In 2020 you received your second master's degree, in Biblical Studies. What was your first degree in and what made you want to continue learning?

Dave: I have an MBA from Rutgers University in professional accounting which broadened my business background and prepared me to meet the requirements of the CPA exam. My initial career was in public accounting followed by corporate roles.

I genuinely enjoy learning and believe you need to continue to grow by exposing yourself to new and different teaching. I must be honest and say that my second master's from Alliance Seminary was so enriching and grew my knowledge of Scripture, but also challenged me. Studying at night for a few hours and squeezing in time for classes stretched me. Late nights in the library are for college guys, not for men whose day job is as an Executive Pastor of a growing church.

I'm thankful that I work in an environment that encourages learning. I want to excite other staff to enjoy being stretched and challenge them to do the same. We all need to be broadened in our understanding of the Word of God as well as a host of other leadership areas.

Bryan: What would you consider to be your strongest quality as a leader?

Dave: To be able to see projects or responsibilities through to completion. Despite obstacles and challenges, I work hard to see and then take the next steps.

Bryan: There are many challenges churches face, especially since the beginning of the pandemic. How have you embraced the popularity of church online, which is becoming such a huge part of someone's life?

Dave: Liquid Church's online team has done a great job of upgrading our church online experience each week. They've worked diligently and explored creative ways to provide a valuable alternative to attending church in-person. I believe this is just the beginning of the support our digital team will make happen. Increasingly, under their leadership, Liquid will be expanding our online offerings and environments.

Bryan: If you could give a piece of advice to anyone reading this book, who may be struggling with their faith, feeling close to God, or even questioning his existence, what would it be?

Dave: It's important to be honest with your doubts and questions, but then it's also vital that you are committed to investing the time to dig deep into the Bible for answers. It's easy for the disappointments and hurts of life to erode our awareness or understanding of the goodness of God and His love. Satan is the "father of lies" and is fighting endlessly to keep each of us from embracing Jesus and continuing to grow in our understanding of His love.

It's so important to remember that how we feel and what we experience does not change the rock-solid reality that God is for you. The cross is the proof that God loves us as demonstrated by His willingness to suffer on the cross. Looking to Jesus and learning about Him is the answer to understanding who God is, how much He loves each of us, and ultimately how you can know who you are and where you fit into God's plan.

Dave is the Executive Pastor of Liquid Church. He oversees ministry services, central leaders and is on the front line of strategic planning. He and his wife, Lois, have three children and four grandchildren.

Clay Thompson

Bryan: You have had quite a journey on your walk with God. When did you first come to know Him?

Clay: Growing up, I was in the church a lot because of my parents. My dad is from North Carolina, so his background is more rigid Southern Baptist. My mom had a unique experience as an immigrant from Cuba. I think her faith played a large part of not only her sponsorship coming to the United States, but also just her walk throughout life being discriminated against in that time.

I grew up in the church and then became a senior intern in high school. I remember sitting in the service as a kid, not going to Sunday school, just sitting, and listening to the actual sermons with them…I think that upbringing ultimately led to me becoming very complacent and then really straying away from the church.

Bryan: At what age did that happen?

Clay: I think it started to happen around high school age, which seems normal because that's when everyone starts to rebel, right? Then in my college years, I just really went off the deep end, just trying to question everything and find who I was apart from the church, my family, my parents, and trying to find my own identity.

Bryan: Were there other reasons you started to question what you learned in church, question how your wider circle of friends who may not have been living with God at the center of their life, and just your own curiosity feed that split?

Clay: I think it was a combination of those and more. One of the main ones was, like you mentioned, just peer pressure and those contradicting ideologies from my friend group. I was at this point in high school where I was oscillating between Christian, which I was born into and then non-Christian, which was my life outside of my family in church. I would go to these awesome, amazing summer retreats and camps, with Young Life and small groups.

I would just be so passionate about my friends there and what we learned. Then I would go to high school, and it was like if I would even mention something about my experiences over the summer, I would get put down for it immediately. Being told that I was in a cult and made fun of for it. I was trying to juggle between these two friend groups, and it was this internal conflict where I was just like, "Okay, well, I can't talk about it anymore in high school, so what do I do? How do I try to bridge the two friend groups?"

Bryan: Were you successful in bridging those friend groups or did one win out over the other?

Clay: Unfortunately, I did cave into peer pressure, and I did end up stepping away because I had known Christianity my whole life. Here was this shiny new life that I was looking at, partying, raving, and drinking and going out. All of the things I despised in high school. When I got to New York City, it was this hustle culture of having a girlfriend, having status, wearing designer clothes, going to the most exclusive venues, being around celebrities and models and having a good career. I put all those things as my "gods" because they were just so enticing to me, and I really caved into that.

Bryan: Based on the interviews in the book and my own experiences, that seems normal. Were you aware of the change occurring?

Clay: I think I was conscious of it deep down, but I chose to really suppress that. I was so distracted by all these new things and experiences, and it was just so consuming that I really didn't think about the consequences. I don't think I had the foresight back then either. When I do things, I just dive headfirst into them. I get very myopic about things, and I have this hyper-focus. I just went headfirst into this new life in New York. I think the city was also an environment for me that was super-conducive to all these different distractions.

It was so hard to just find a grounding place and equilibrium to get away from all that. I was just constantly bombarded and consumed by all these pressures every day. I just knew I had all of this sudden popularity and social mobility now that I didn't have in high school, and I didn't want to look back.

It was pretty a stark contrast from going from my Christian life to my non-Christian life. It was a firm line in the sand from where I was a senior intern, even having given the sermons in front of the congregation a few times.

I remember the one sermon I gave that resonated with me, which is part of the reason why I changed my name ultimately, was the jars of clay in the Bible, and filling the jars of clay with things that aren't fulfilling, about holding a void vacant in our lives.

Ironically, that's exactly what I had ended up ultimately doing. But for that year that I was a senior intern, we had to sign a contract, a social contract to not drink or party or do drugs or have sex or anything.

That whole year, me and my close small group of friends that were interns, who I'm still friends with, we didn't do any of that. It was one of the best years of my life. It was the calm before the storm.

I got into the only school I applied to in New York. It was Parsons [School of Design] or bust. And as soon as I got into school, it was just, like I said, off the deep end. I just started doing everything I could. The unofficial name given to our class by the tabloids that year was "Hard partying hippie school."

Bryan: What was your family's reaction to the change in you and at what point did you realize that you had to go back to your way of life?

Clay: I think I was a functional Christian at that point in New York. To me that was more dangerous than my family having a full grasp of what I was going through and what I was doing in the city. It allowed me to become complacent in a way where I could still present myself as the same person that I was pre-New York to my family, my church, and my friends when I would come back and visit.

But then I was living an entirely separate life and managing to balance these extreme ups and downs enough where I was just functional. That was worse because to me, it just allowed me to go down this dark place without showing any significant symptoms or signs of it on the outside, at least not at that point.

I went to Parsons and my roommate went to NYU. We shared campuses, we roomed together, shared friend groups and social events, and we had grown up in church together. We were both going through the same experience in the city. I remember there was a conversation I had, a few months into college. My friend and I were dissecting our lives and our friends' lives back home, that either were still at home or were from church.

We came to the naive conclusion back then that we were living a life that was far more fulfilling than any of their lives because of all the things that we were doing. We were like, "They have a really boring life. They are just not living life to its fullest potential. We feel sorry for them." This was our mentality at that point, living in this magical world of excess and infinite potential. It was adult Disneyland.

Bryan: Even as strong as my walk is now, the few times I have gone to the city, the "everything goes" mentality comes to the forefront for me.

Clay: In New York I was celebrated. It felt like the sin that I racked up were tokens, feeling like I had more street cred with all my friends. I became a ringleader, to the point that even my most secular friends had a hard time keeping up.

I had this dark moment in New York. I was in school, and I was skipping classes and I was barely showing up at this point. I was just going out and partying, finding the next "move" and waking up at 3 p.m. every day just to make it to my studio class in the afternoon and barely be present for it.

I just bull-shitted my way through everything. Then I realized I didn't want to be in school. I was bored and my ambitions had transcended my pace of life. So, I dropped out and I started doing my own thing, I started going even faster, but I was just so lost at that point and didn't realize it. I was left with the remnants of a seemingly perfect life, trying to hold together the pieces by chasing the next high.

I realized my environment was super-toxic. The friends I had were toxic and I just felt this anxiety that was accumulating. That eventually manifested in the form of a panic attack, which turned into an anxiety disorder, which led me to ultimately move to Hawaii. I needed to just be alone, breathe, reconnect, find myself and find what was wrong with me because I had no idea what was going on in my head or my life at that point.

Bryan: Professionally, you were in an industry where you are working on campaigns that may not have aligned with your Christian upbringing, but fed the life you were creating in New York City, right?

Clay: That was a large part of it. It was not until recently that I have been able to really find conviction in the Bible, what I believe and stand firm in that and start to really move away from those friends and that type of work. The more I move away from it, God just keeps blessing those decisions tenfold.

But back then when I was in New York, five, six years ago, I was presented with what seemed like big opportunities. A few of those opportunities were working for artists for Sony and Epic Records and telling their story. I would interview the talent to find out more about them, the direction they wanted to go in and the campaigns they wanted me to create.

There was one artist that had a huge following and had success early on in his career. He started shifting his image, his brand, and his campaign deeply toward mysticism, witchcraft. I remember sitting there and I was just thinking, "This guy is really cool, and this is such a big opportunity for me". At the same time, it was weird sitting here listening to him, because this was literally everything that I was ever taught not to believe in growing up, from a Cuban mother.

That was where the conflict really started. I was working so hard because I just had so many ambitions, that I tolerated so much and put so many morals and beliefs aside to just pursue those opportunities. I burnt myself out, which led to the panic attack eventually. I think it was more than the work itself. It was this spiritual warfare inside of me just going back and forth between the world and then who I was.

Bryan: You are 25, which puts you into a generation that is not as open to living a Christ-centered life in a world of "you do you and I'll do me". Did going through the struggles you went through at such a young age make you be more compassionate with people who are struggling with identity?

Clay: Yes and no. No, because I struggled. Parsons is a very liberal art school. It's a beautiful freak show of the world's top talent. I remember the first day of class, the first question they asked us, which I had never heard before or was familiar with, was what our personal gender pronoun was? Everyone there knew what it meant, and they were expected to give theirs.

It was different, and I was more conservative and had more conservative friends. But I loved it because it was this place where everyone, like you said, was celebrated, could be free, could be themselves. I thought that was so awesome because the town I grew up in was not the most accepting place of everyone.

That period did help me be compassionate now because I was able to question what I believed, then solidify that identity and then remain compassionate toward the people that didn't identify with those beliefs. It was a process of loving everyone but putting myself aside, and then pushing everyone away for my change in beliefs, and then ultimately standing firm in what I believe, and learning how to balance that with loving other people.

Bryan: I have had quite the journey with how I identify in terms of sexuality, since my relationship with God came to the forefront of my life. Did you, or anyone you know, struggle with the same thing?

Clay: When I was in Hawaii, there was a time when I was at my lowest low, and I ended up going to this small men's group at a friend's apartment with young guys from Hope Chapel Church. One of the guys in the group was a non-practicing "gay" and was also one of the most charismatic, wise, theologically knowledgeable, and funny guys in our group. When I first went to the group, I noticed an obvious distinction in his personality. I never witnessed that in the church because I had never been in an environment where people were so accepting of that. When I was there, I didn't know how to approach him because I didn't know him, but I wanted to know more about his experience.

I didn't want to be rude, and I just waited until he shared his experiences openly, which inspired me to leave behind the partying, drugs, etc. and that scene myself, because I realized this kid was funny, was such a light, was so open and he was one of the strongest leaders in our group. He would lead Bible study for the middle school every week. And he was just such an amazing follower of Jesus, abiding by God's laws and denting himself of all urges and temptations, but he was also just his unapologetic self at the same time. It was such an inspiration to me because I realized I didn't have to hide who I was to anyone.

I like to dance, I like to be the life of the party, to rally people and make sure everyone is having a good time. I like to make people laugh and go out and facilitate it all and there's nothing wrong with that, within reason and within limits and the right context. I can still live a godly life and be an example without giving up the fun, energetic, loving person I am. For the first time in my life that clicked, and I was like, "Okay, I can be who God made me to be, and I don't have to be ashamed of that and still advocate for my faith."

Recently, I was having a conversation with one of my best friends, who is gay and an atheist. I asked if he was going to the pride parade and he said he wasn't because although he is gay, he did not need to wave around a flag because it is just a small part of who he is, not his full identity.

We started talking about Christianity and the controversial topic of how homosexuality is viewed within the church. He told me he did not agree with Christianity because they were not accepting and hated gay people. I told him that simply was not true, and he said that was all he heard. I told him I thought that was unfortunate and asked if he had gone into the Bible and read what it said? He said he had not and started referencing things out of context from the Bible based on what he had heard.

I think that is a problem with some churches because they misinterpret by pulling parts of scripture out. I believe that is one of the biggest enemies of the church because then we get people like my friend who's liberal and wants to be accepting of everyone and is highly ethical and thinks that the Christian community contradicts those philosophies, when in fact, the love and acceptance we show is a fundamental part of what we believe as Christians. Our collective societal morality is based on a Judeo-Christian foundation.

I was brought up and taught to live in Jesus' footsteps and that is to love everyone. So, while I am no longer going out and partying, drinking the way I was, or attending a pride parade, it does not mean that I do not accept and love everyone. I believe that is the way someone who feels marginalized by the church, is to be examples of who Jesus is, to love everyone like He loves us. It's only through relationship that we can share God's truth.

I think the brother I had in Maui confirmed that ideology inside of me. And since then, it's just been this journey to accept myself first and then to accept other people through God's example of love.

Bryan: Tell me more about your decision to move to Hawaii.

Clay: I was in New York and like I said, I'd put everything in these counterfeit "gods", but not the real God. Being so young, I thought I had everything. I had two offices, on 5th Avenue by Central Park and in Tribeca that I was paying for monthly. I had a small team of people and two interns that I was managing as part of my own production company. I had large contracts. I had a billionairess and high fashion designer as a girlfriend, and then I didn't have a girlfriend, then I was just serial dating.

I had a best friend who was my business partner, and then I did not. I was also taking Adderall, which started as an innocent, subtle supplement to my work and social life and then became a huge dependency. I was snorting lines of Adderall constantly to stay up three to four nights at a time with sometimes brief power naps in between just to work and then to socialize and then to party, and then drinking and smoking to mellow out and try to sleep and come down from that. I did not even rest when I was sick. I was on Adderall for entire family vacations. I was on this constant high, spreading myself thin and making an appearance everywhere all at once. But it was so normalized in NYC. Sleep was a commodity, a luxury and a reward for the weak.

Bryan: It is a vicious cycle.

Clay: It was a vicious cycle that I could not get out of. I had enough self-awareness to realize that this lifestyle wasn't sustainable long-term. I knew I needed to cut this stuff off, but the problem was that I had been operating in fifth gear for so long. I didn't know how to get out of it. I had forgotten how to breathe, how to sit down, how to be still. I defied my own nature until I had conditioned myself to become someone unrecognizable, a machine.

I went to a friend's wedding down in Annapolis who was in the Navy. Everyone was drinking a lot at a party on one of the islands after that wedding. I was at a point where I hadn't slept in three days, and I had given up all substances very recently. I didn't have anything to bring me down. I was anxious, and I had this tension in my back. I was trying to take a nap and I was frustrated that I could not fall asleep. The night after the wedding, we were all drinking at this party, and I drank an entire bottle of whiskey myself and it didn't do anything. I wasn't drunk. I was like, "What is this? I just feel nothing right now. I'm so numb." I continued to drink the rest of the night, just kept drinking, drinking, drinking trying to feel a remnant of something, anything. And nothing, just nothing.

The next morning, we were driving back to NJ, and I started floating out of my body, I had no idea what was going on. I thought I was dying, but I hadn't smoked or taken anything.

I was sober and was having this out of body experience and did not know what was going on, so I started praying and asking God what was going on, pleading with Him to get me through this, just crying. My friends in the car had no idea what was going on. I thought it was just a terrible hangover because I had blacked out, which was a common and familiar occurrence for me. But this was different. Now I know that was my first panic attack. Everything from that point changed.

A series of events that stemmed from that led to undiagnosed agoraphobia. I could not leave the house; I could not drive past the end of the street or walk more than 50 feet from my car. I could not get in the car with other people or go on runs. It debilitated every part of my life as an independent and adventurous person. I am a pilot, yet I could no longer get on a plane without blacking out from panic.

My love and outlet was downhill mountain biking and snowboarding. I had traveled to Taiwan on a whim to bike the circumference of the island in three weeks without a tour or any experience only two months prior, and now I could not even get on a ski or bike lift without crying. I felt as if my limbs were cut off, I thought I might be stuck like this for the rest of my life, paralyzed with fear, living in a shell of a person I once knew, with no explanation for why or what was happening.

That cumulative experience ultimately led to my decision of moving to Hawaii. I was depressed and sick for months through Christmas, in a meaningless relationship and trying to hang on to my previous life while drinking the anxiety away. I needed and wanted desperately to get away from all these triggers and emotions and all those new and damaging connections I had made in my mind.

So here I was in Maui, with nothing more than a backpack and a plane ticket. A fresh start. I left all of my worries behind to rot. I was up in the rainforest building tiny homes with my friend for four months, and I didn't have shoes, I didn't have a shirt, I did not have a phone and we were eating beans out of a can over a fire. We were getting water out of a well and living in a muddy, flooded and spider- and cockroach-ridden tent. I thought, "This is great. Exactly what I needed. I've given up everything in my life to find God, this is where I'm going to find Him." Then I realized I was completely empty, and it was even worse than before because now, I didn't have the substances. I didn't have the outlets that I had in New York to express my frustrations. But in New York, I also didn't have any friends around me that were Christian. I didn't have a support system. And neither did I have it here. I didn't have a church.

It's like I had taken my glass filled with dirty water, I had dumped it out, and then it was just empty. There was nothing in it. And so, I eventually moved out of the rainforest, to civilization. I got a job working for a doctor during the Covid pandemic treating VIPs on vacation, and then serving and bartending and photographing weddings and influencers. And being around that culture led me right back into the drinking and partying again, beach parties that went viral on the news and social media and private parties with countless celebrities. And I remember the anxiety started to creep up again, in a way where it was so bad that I'd get up in the morning and it would just be the first thing in the morning, I'd start the day with an anxiety attack.

Bryan: Panic attacks can be terrifying because you think you are having a heart attack.

Clay: It is terrifying because I didn't want to go to sleep, I didn't want to wake up. It got to the point, while I would never commit suicide, and I was not thinking about actively killing myself, but I was scared where the thought would just pass my mind quickly in more of an intuitive feeling than a fully developed thought. Where logically, I was thinking/feeling, "Well, if this is my life every day, it's exhausting. I am just going through the motions of life. Not enjoying anything, just trying to get through the next panic attack, completely numb, wearing a mask, then what's the point of being here?"

I was just drowning that growing feeling out with drinking, and the friends I had in Hawaii were even worse than the ones in the city in terms of their pace of life. Hawaii is this secret place where you can do whatever you want, and no one can tell you what to do. These billionaires go out and seek refuge in sin out there. I was part of that and that was bad. I was treading water, I could not live in my head, which used to be my comfort zone, and I was scared to go surf or fly.

I remember there was this one point where I called my family and I had thought about my brother, Robert, for the first time in a long time. I started crying and I was like, "I just want to be with Robert." I had never thought that before. I was like, "Why am I thinking this? Why do I suddenly want to be really close with Robert and my family?" I called my mom, and I asked her, "How's Robert doing? Is he okay?" She said that he was okay, but that he missed me and wished that I would come back home. I got off the phone and I have never felt more empty or low in my life. Just lonely and completely alone.

I went to the beach, and I got on my knees next to some sea turtles, and I just started praying and I felt ridiculous. I looked up at the sky and I just started talking to God and questioning everything. Sitting in paradise under the stars and I could not appreciate any of it.

There was a photographer on the island, Cyrus, who some of my friends at the time preferred not to work with because he was so openly Christian. I ended up calling him and telling him I was not in a great place mentally.

He said how crazy it was that I had called him because I had crossed his mind. We had only met once via Instagram. He was going through his own minor issues in life that he was vulnerable about with me and said that he wanted to get his guy's church/friend group together and invited me to join them that week. I walked into one of the guy's apartments in Maui, sat down with the guys and just openly told them everything that I had been through. They immediately accepted and encouraged and uplifted me. This huge weight was just lifted off me.

Bryan: Liquid Church has a huge heart to serve those with special needs. I had the privilege of serving at this year's prom and it was such an incredible experience. The thing that really struck me was that my sole thought was to go in there, work as a buddy and make sure he/she had the most amazing, fun night.

My buddy did, but what I was not expecting, was that serving that night my buddy would also give me a massive gift, which was the gift of laughter, dancing, and the pure joy and happiness that I had not been feeling since the loss of my brother five weeks prior. I know your brother, Robert, has also had great experiences at the prom. What does your relationship with him mean to you?

Clay: I had the privilege of being an aid and a teacher at a special needs organization that Robert was a part of before I moved to NYC. Unfortunately, they've closed because of Covid.

I remember when I was applying for the job, I had no idea that I would find what you just talked about, which was that transformation in my own life, being closer to them. After working with special needs and disabled adults for a couple months and working with Robert closely, I realized that Robert's love and their love is probably closer to God's example of love than anyone else could emulate because they have no real judgment or boundaries or authority to put anyone down because they just are who they are, full of Agape love.

Bryan: A 100 percent authentic life.

Clay: Exactly, and so that was an example for me because I was not living a 100 percent authentic life. I looked at my brother and I looked at the other people in the program and I realized the incongruity between the two of us. I realized I started to see my brother as a reflection. Because of that, I started to pull away from him and I started to push him away subtly.

That's when I moved to Hawaii, and I tried to ignore him. It wasn't because I didn't want to be with him. It wasn't because I didn't care about him. It is because I care about him so much that it hurt.

I needed to find myself without that burden weighing on me. I had suppressed that hurt so deep down that here he was just loving me, and I could not return it. Don't take this the wrong way because I don't mean to compare my brother to a dog, but he mimicked a dog who just loves you unconditionally. You could have a horrible day and be bitter, but when you come home your dog is always there waiting for you, to love you. I did not feel I could love him back in the same way because I was so caught up in what I was dealing with. And that's how I felt.

That is why I think he was instrumental in bringing me to my knees when I was in Hawaii, in a way. When I looked at my own life, I realized my brother did not understand why I was not with him and was 3,000 miles away. He was just living his life trying to love as best as he knows how.

Bryan: Now that you are back, I imagine your relationship is the strongest it has ever been.

Clay: For sure. One of those reasons is because of the Division of Developmental Disabilities (DDD) and public partnerships. Great resources and programs that allocate a predetermined budget upon approval and circumstance, for individuals with disabilities, like Robert, each year for extracurricular programs and care. The program that he was going to unfortunately shut down during Covid. Through public partnerships however, a family can designate a member of the family or a friend as a caretaker/aid. That person then spends time educating them and doing things that are productive, educational, and fun. I started coming up with activities for us to do together, like cooking, shopping for groceries we needed for the meals, taking our dog for walks, going to the beach, museum, working out, going on hikes or to the zoo, etc.

Bryan: Do you think your relationship with Robert is the most genuine one you have in your life?

Clay: Definitely. There are things I do with Robert, like making funny noises or voices while we are driving together that I would never do with anyone else. I also think Robert and members of the special needs community have almost like a sixth sense, but it is spiritual, not physical. It is also intuitive, where Robert can just pick up the energy in a room and he knows exactly what is going on. He may communicate in his own way, but he knows how people are, how they work and who they truly are. You cannot get a thing past Robert. He is very emotionally intelligent.

I have a good intuition myself, but I just don't listen to it. Because of that, I have gotten into terrible situations in the past and in relationships that were not good for me. Robert is loving with everyone, and with my last girlfriend he was so standoffish and distant toward her. My family and I talked about it and how he picked up on everything that I was not seeing and had chosen to negate. I often joke that I am going to bring him to my business meetings … standing in a large boardroom: "What do you think Robert, deal or no deal?" Robert: "Nope!" Me: "Sorry guys, better luck next time."

Robert has become so much more than a person that I have to "take care of" and has actually been the one taking care of me in many ways. He has been an anchor for me. Someone who watches out for and protects me. I would make a lot more stupid decisions if it were not for him.

Bryan: Now that you are back in New Jersey, you have been immersing yourself at Liquid; joining my men's small group, the production team, etc. What do you see as God's future for your life?

Clay: Community is a huge part of it. I believe that is very important. The longer that I postpone having people with God at the center of their life, the longer I postpone the purpose God has for me.

I have been distracted for so long with things that are superficial and worldly. I think many of my friends have become complacent in the same way, which is frustrating to witness. I am finally starting to see what God has in store for all of us, but I realize I cannot change anyone if they do not want it for themselves. I need to change myself first and love by example.

I am politely distancing myself from them because I realized I need strong Christians to hold me accountable to grow and become a leader, so being part of a church community is a huge part of what I am trying to seek more of.

Beyond that, I am trying to find ways that I can use my creative gifts and love for community and storytelling to glorify God. I know that if I do that, those gifts will be blessed tenfold, because God is the one who has given me the talents and propensities that I possess.

Bryan: Any inclination that He may be calling you into a pastoral role?

Clay: I mentioned this to my mom and then briefly to Pastor Tim. Being a pastor is the last thing I would have ever considered for my life. I would have actively run away from it like it was a plague. I had not ever aspired to be a lead pastor on a platform or stage. But I have so many ideas and projects and stories to tell that I am open in whatever format God wants me to use those. Pastor Tim has set a great example of how that can look beyond the stigmatized pastoral role. Who knows if that's God's will for me one day. I'm not running so much anymore.

In the conversation with my mom, I told her that I think I was trying to please both of my worlds for so long, that there was a point where I was trying to find wisdom in the Bible, which I actively am. But I was also trying to justify the wisdom I found in the world so that I could continue to fit in and be celebrated.

Then I realized I was just diluting God's truth with a worldly perspective. I should not be leaning on anything else but Him. In doing that I have the responsibility and obligation to myself to take a stance in what I believe. That may mean I am going to offend a lot of my worldly friends and I have accepted that. I realize that is a part of my journey moving forward and I am starting to get more comfortable with that.

To that end I have an iPad that I carry around and I write on. I have over 20 journals because I have so many ideas all the time that I would make myself insane if I could not write them down and organize them.

One of the ideas I have came from the isolation I felt while living in Hawaii. When I was in New York, I was using a really popular app all the time for client work. It is like Photoshop for your phone. While I was in Hawaii I was working for a doctor and this guy we were working with was going through similar anxiety. It was crazy how our experiences aligned. We started talking about his being a designer while I was giving him an IV and he was asking me about my design work. He says his name is …. " and I said, "as in the guy who developed and founded the "app that I used while living in New York that I wished I could one day meet?"

We started talking and I came to find out that he grew up with the founder of the Bible app, Bobby Gruenewald. He was completely vulnerable with me about his life and experience and his journey learning to breathe and pray. Having met someone on the island to talk with about design reignited a passion and flame in me that had started to dim. I remember we would get together at 4:30 every morning at his house in Hawaii and watch the sunrise and just breathe and pray together. Sometimes we wouldn't say a word and I would just leave afterward. Sometimes we would stay there talking for hours. I can only imagine what his family thought once they came back and watched us out the window doing this. His kids probably thought we were crazy, doing handstands and breathing to loud music.

The reason I say all of this is because we were working on developing a breathing and journaling app. When I came back from Hawaii, I realized I had to learn how to just breathe and pray on my own. That became a huge part of my recovery from anxiety and then all the substances I had been taking.

I have two apps that I use on my iPad every morning. One is Stoic, which is a mental health tracking app, and the other is the Bible App. I always go to the Stoic app first. It asks me what I want to focus on that day and then it populates a list. You click on what you want, and it will present prompts based off the areas you chose. I would always write it all down and it really helped me. It also had a breathing exercise that I would do that would prepare and prime me for reading my devotional. But then I realized if the Bible app is the full and only truth, why am I using Stoic first. For me and many of my friends that are secular, the Bible is a scary and intimidating book. It seems boring, but it's not. I do realize the Bible is a big and intimidating book where people don't even know where to start. On top of that there are pastors and churches that are misinterpreting it and taking things out of context. I think being able to destigmatize the Bible and bringing it to my generation in this digital age, would be so impactful.

I think we take the Bible in little pieces way too often as opposed to seeing it as an all-encompassing book. I think the underlying story is that God loves us, and He tells us that every day. He loves us so much that He sent His only son to die for us. I think when people can finally and fully grasp that, it washes away any other false narrative that people have. You realize I can be who I am, and there's still a higher being that loves me for that.

I think that knowledge can help everyone, Christian or not. You could be any religion. You could be atheist. But everyone has the same desires and needs in common and that is to be loved.

Bryan: One of the biggest events in my life that put me on my current path was my baptism as an adult at Liquid. What was the difference for you with being baptized as a baby versus as an adult?

Clay: I didn't really understand what baptism meant, to be honest, leading up to my second baptism as an adult, which was my choice. One brother that I am particularly close with, who has a similar past to mine, was part of my small group in Hawaii. He welcomed me and accepted me from day one. His name is Sam. He told me if baptism was something I really wanted to do, we should get the guys together, talk it over and then pray about it. I remember they were sending me passages and verses and things that I had never read before, putting into perspective what baptism really meant.

That experience that I got leading up to my baptism, of what it meant, was not this out of body, spiritual, supernatural, shift or experience where suddenly, you go underwater and then you are this super-Christian. I don't believe that, although some may feel differently.

But I do believe that it's a personal and a deeply private covenant between you and God. Then at the same time, you want people that you can trust on a deep level around you, witnessing what you're going through, witnessing that private, intimate moment that you have with God, and keeping you accountable. I really felt baptism was the last chance for me to move forward to try to live with God. It was literally the last resort for me. I really wanted to do it and leave my old life behind.

When I got baptized it was amazing. I did it on the beach in Maui. It was very early in the morning, at like 4 a.m. with four of the guys that were strong Christians in the group. They had practically just met me. They were creatives like me, which was very cool. They prayed over me before they dunked me. One of them recorded the whole thing and made an edit out of it, so I get to look back on it anytime I want as a reminder.

Whatever I do in life now, and I may mess up sometimes, but I look back and realize I am not the person I was before that moment, not because I was dunked in water, but because I actively made the decision to live a different life after that.

Bryan: To that end, earlier you briefly mentioned that you changed your name to Clay from Jose. That is a huge thing to do. What is the story behind doing so?

Clay: When I moved to Hawaii, I changed my name from Jose to Clay, not for any negative or shameful reason. I'm actually very proud of my birth name, which is José Manuél Columbié Thompson, which was my grandfather's name. It was really a symbol for myself, not for anyone else, to signify the shift in my life and my decision-making from New York to Hawaii. I had such bad experiences during that time of my life that I was leading in New York, that I wanted to just wash clean anything that was associated with it. It was just refreshing and nice to be starting from a blank slate.

In New York, the first thing everyone asks you is where do you work? Where'd you go to school? What do you do? In Hawaii people look down on you if those are the things that you talk about. I really appreciated that no one cared what I did, and no one cared where I went to school. My whole identity was wiped clean because I had nothing to really talk about other than who I was as an authentic person.

Being named Clay really helped me in being able to distinguish between that and then slowly build up my new identity in God. Beyond that, it's just had significance symbolically throughout my life that is reoccurring.

Clay is a designer, editor, producer and the owner of Clay Collective (https://www.claythompson.art/). But his most important roles are as a child of God, a mentor, and caregiver to his brother, Robert, who is part of the special needs community.

Bryan: You have one of the most beautiful relationships with God I have ever seen. When did you become aware of how much He loved you?

Sydney: I was fortunate enough to be raised by wonderful parents who instilled prayer into my daily ritual, and they took me to church on Sundays since I was little. People would say that they could see my love for God from a very young age, so I believe that the seed was always within me. It was all beyond comprehension because of my age. That all changed when I was 10 years old. I had a conversation with my parents regarding my diagnosis from birth, which they tried to shield me from. The conversation was filled with a lot of questions on my end and a lot of tears on theirs.

A few months later, I began experiencing persistent headaches that wouldn't go away, which led my parents to take me to get testing done. Those tests revealed that I needed to be admitted into the hospital for brain surgery immediately. It was something that my parents nor I was expecting, so it was absolutely devastating. Learning of my diagnosis, then having to face brain surgery, took a great toll on me. It was in those moments of my fear, questioning and doubt that I began to pray like never before because I knew that the surgery was not something I could face on my own. It wasn't until I was being wheeled down to the operating room that I felt this wave of peace come over me, which was something that I never felt. It was made so clear in that moment that I wasn't going to be facing the surgery alone, I was going to be facing it with my Heavenly Father by my side. That was the first time that He revealed His love for me that I was aware of. It sometimes takes the most devastating and lonely times to realize how powerful His love is. Ever since then, the evidence of His love has always been made so clear to me and my love for Him is beyond what words could express. I just want to go tell the world about Jesus!

Bryan: You write beautifully, which is a talent He gave you. How does it feel to know your words have such an impact on people?

Sydney: Do they have an impact on people? Well, if they do it is such an honor to know that. I never would have thought this would happen especially given the fact that writing was something I struggled a lot with at one point. To hold a pen was such an effort, never did I think then that I would be able to type like I am able to now. It was only through God's sufficient grace and the persistence of my family and many therapists that I got to this point.

As I began learning how to type, the Holy Spirit began to move and still moves in a way that I never thought was possible. I have always known that it is the Holy Spirit moving because when I have an intention to write, I never know what I am going to write about, and when I begin it all flows with such ease. By the time I am finished, I am more often than not surprised at myself. That is pure evidence that they are not my words, but they are the Holy Spirit's words. So, it is awesome to see how the Holy Spirit is moving through the words I type to impact the lives of others.

Bryan: What do you draw from when you are writing?

Sydney: The situations in life sometimes take over and I fall into the valley of my faith. While I am in the valley, I look back on my writings and I see how the Holy Spirit manifested within me, which is a steppingstone that is so needed to climb back up to the mountaintop of my faith. So, I believe that God allows me to pour His word out not only for the sake of reaching others, but for an instrumental tool in my own walk with Him. It gives me great joy knowing that my gift of writing is used on so many different levels.

Bryan: You and I serve together at Liquid Church, which is known for their heart for the special needs community. How does it feel to belong to a church where you are seen and not pushed aside?

Sydney: First and foremost, it is such an honor to serve beside you! Prior to attending Liquid Church, there was very little feeling of knowing that I was understood and heard as I have faced challenges fitting into a society where there was no one I could relate to. Upon attending and learning that several pastors had their own children with special needs and their passion for the special needs community there provided such a strong sense of belonging. Little did I know the doors that it would open for me and the lessons that it would teach me being a part of a church with such great passion. The special needs community in which I had very little knowledge about has now taught me so much. I never imagined it to be a community so big. I have discovered my great passion of helping those in need by attending "Night to Shine", which is a prom for special needs individuals that was hosted several times by our church in conjunction with the Tim Tebow Foundation. I knew my passion was so deep from the second I stepped my foot in the door as I saw so many individuals, including myself, get the VIP treatment.

Although I loved every second of it, my eyes were opened to so much more. The happiness that illuminated across the room was where my focus was, and it has enriched my heart in such a way that I now know that the importance of giving back is something near and dear to my heart. Beyond that, several of the pastors have asked my input on things, which has made me feel that my opinion mattered. All these things have been steppingstones that have led me to feeling a strong sense of validation.

Prior to attending Liquid Church, I had never realized how much I lacked the sense of validation, as I now know that it wasn't a feeling that has ever been felt. I am so grateful to God for leading me to this church to open my eyes to the things that are so essential for me as I navigate the gift of life that He has so freely given me.

Bryan, as I tell you all the time, when I am in church, I never want to leave!!! I know that you feel the same way!!

Bryan: Anyone who knows you would say that your personality sparkles brighter than the Times Square ball that drops on New Year's Eve. How do you stay so positive, upbeat, happy, and kind in a world that may not always be kind to you in return?

Sydney: Bryan, I am so flattered by that first statement!!! But it is the Holy Spirit leading me to see the blessing in situations. That is what keeps me so positive, upbeat, happy, and kind. It is also the way that I look at every situation. The negativity in every situation is great and there is always room for dwelling and questioning and I sometimes fall into that trap, but there is also room to see the blessing in every situation, which is why I make every effort to see it. That comes with ease because of the Holy Spirit's leading. The seasons that I fall into the trap of negativity often occur when I shy away from going to church because of life's circumstances getting in the way. Church is the only place I get fed with the knowledge of God's word, which gives the Holy Spirit's leading something to drive off of.

I look at the world surrounding me and the people surrounding me who treat me in a negative way, and I wonder what is going on in their lives that is making them so bitter. I may not know what is going on, but I do know that the only solution for each one of them is for them to come to know God. With knowing the solution, I make every effort to pray for them. I will honestly say that praying for those who treat you in such a way takes a great deal of effort, but if Jesus could recklessly love and forgive those who nailed him to the Cross and pray for his enemies so can I.

Bryan: What is your favorite scripture verse and why?

Sydney: I have so many Bible verses that I absolutely love, but the one that I live by throughout all my days is Philippians 4:13, which says, "I can do all things through Christ who strengthens me". It speaks such few words, but those words are so profound, and they are so touching to me. As I navigate the everyday life, my strength with things that I have to endure and face sometimes wears thin and the desire to give up creeps in and that is when I need the reminder to stop relying on my own strength. I have to rely on the strength that only Jesus can give me, and I am so thankful for the promise of His strength as it has carried me through many things. It has given me the motivation to face each day knowing that I can do exceedingly abundant and wonderful things through my days because of it.

150

Bryan: Will you ever get used to hearing that you inspire people?

Sydney: Hearing that I inspire people is something I will never take for granted but it is a great blessing to hear as I feel I am doing something beautiful not only for them, not only for myself, but for God because He has called us to go forth and help those in need. He has called us to speak of his name in times such as we are living in. By hearing that, I feel as though I am doing God's calling.

Aside from feeling that I am doing God's calling, I have come to realize throughout my life that inspiration in the lives of others is so important because what we see on the surface doesn't tell the full story of what is going on beneath it. So maybe inspiration gives some people the motivation to face each day with a positive outlook. I also love inspiring others for that reason.

Bryan: Do you have interest in becoming a pastor?

Sydney: There is a strong desire within me, and it would be a great blessing if that is God's calling for me. I am trusting in His calling and if that is the way he wants me to go, He will reveal it to me. But if it doesn't happen, I will be just as satisfied doing my part in magnifying His name and leading generations to him by spreading His word. Some of you reading this may be wondering, "Why do I have to wait on God's calling? Why can't you just do it if you have a desire for it?" The reason is that I have always known that God has had a calling on my life and He has revealed that to me so many times. As I have gone by Him leading me, those things have always worked for my benefit and for His glory. I have done things without His revelation and those things have never worked out for my favor nor for His glory. It makes the fact clear that I can't do such things within my own flesh, I need my Heavenly Father to lead the way.

Bryan: What are some examples of when you have been discriminated against and how did you handle the challenges that come along with that?

Sydney: I will say that there is an emotional toll and roller coaster that comes with having special needs, and throughout my school years that is what I went through, as there was a longing within me to do the things that other children could do, but I unfortunately couldn't.

Their days were spent playing sports and mine were spent being pulled out of classes for therapies, which was such an awkward feeling. There was no common ground, which resulted in me feeling so sad. It was made perfectly clear how some of the other kids felt about me through incidents that arose on the horizon where I was judged based on my appearance and the way I did things. My glasses were knocked off during those incidents. Things never went beyond that because the right people were told, which was a blessing in disguise. After enduring these incidents, I was left feeling deeply hurt as there was nothing I could do to prevent them from happening again and knowing how cruel some kids could be instead of lending a helping hand. I am so grateful that nothing more has occurred, and I wouldn't trade my childhood, my weaknesses nor the incidents that occurred because those years of enduring all that I did has made me a better person.

Bryan: What would you like to say about the special needs community to those that are reading this?

Sydney: By my own experiences and being a part of the special needs community, I have learned that there are things that many take for granted, that the struggle goes a little deeper when having special needs. The skills of persistence, confidence, self-worth, and determination are so essential. If my time wasn't spent with learning how to build those skills in the many years of therapies, there would be no way I would be where I am today. I will openly say that it is a journey, but anything can be achieved if the mind is set to it.

As I look at my peers, I look at them beyond their label, beyond their category, beyond their weaknesses and I look at their unique journey they have traveled to get to where they are today. Without our Heavenly Father's presence, there is no way that the skills of persistence, self-worth, confidence, and determination would have a standing chance. Some may lack the ability to fathom His presence within them or even know Him, but it is my belief that if life has to be navigated in such a way our forgiving, loving Heavenly Father plants a seed within them so that they have every tool that is needed to flourish in every way.

The special needs community is often forgotten about, which makes sadness settle within them because people on the outside do not want to take the time to look in and they assume that there is no purpose for them. But if the initiative is taken to look in, I am telling you that you will be surprised. They will teach you things beyond imagination as my peers have taught me.

It is up to the people on the outside to let the special needs community shine. I strongly encourage you to look into their world and make it known that they have a purpose. You may have to be a little more patient with some of the individuals. Do not let your first attempt discourage you if you think that they are beyond reach because I am telling you that throughout my encounters that the first attempt brings them such joy and enriches their lives. They just may need the time to master their skills to respond back to you in their own unique way. Look beyond their label, category, "weakness" and look deeper within them and at their unique journey as I do. Be the reason for them to shine in your life. Value the lessons they teach you and allow them to enrich your life.

Sydney and CeeJay are a brother and sister who share a special bond. Sydney works at The Clean Water Café at Liquid Church.

CeeJay Larino

Bryan: How do you navigate the challenges of being in college and being a Christian?

CeeJay: As a college student, there are a plethora of challenges that all students face on a daily basis. More than just the rigor of academics, there are posing challenges that students face in the social aspect of their lives. One of the biggest challenges for me is standing firm in my beliefs when everyone around me contradicts my reasoning. As a person, I always try to use reasoning and logic to establish a point of view. Whether that be in religion, politics, or just a mere stance on any topic. Practicality is my priority.

The difficult part in having your own opinions is internal. I think it's natural for everyone to want to express their beliefs and have everyone think the way they do, but in today's culture, it seems that our differences divide us more than our similarities unite us. As someone who wants to get along with everyone, I keep my beliefs to myself unless someone asks me about them. I feel that keeping my beliefs to myself will get me further and allow me to build relationships even in a world of intolerance. I've learned this through countless debates over various topics that usually end poorly. More than this, there are pressures that I face daily, as well. The challenge may be putting all your effort into studying for an exam, or it may also be a group of people doing something that makes you feel uncomfortable. Regardless of what the challenge may pose, I rely on God for it all. When situations go my way, I thank God. When situations don't go my way, I also thank God. It's comforting to know that there is nothing I cannot overcome because God is on my side, which makes challenges not as daunting.

Bryan: Your sister, Sydney, is one of the most beautiful souls on Earth. How challenging was it for you as a brother to see people be mean to her because of her special needs?

CeeJay: As Sydney's brother, I can say that without a doubt Sydney is the backbone of our family. Obviously, as her brother, I see her in a different light that not everyone else sees her in. I've seen her achievements and struggles, her highs and lows, her happiness and pain — I've seen it all. Whatever storm we had to weather, we weathered together. By having the opportunity to be by her side through triumph and tribulation, it only allows me to think the world of her. So, with this preconception in my head that my sister is everything, it destroys me when people treat her like anything less than royalty.

It takes a special kind of person to have the patience, amiability, and compassion to do as much as talk with Sydney, and I recognize that not everyone has these qualities. I struggle coming to the realization that not everyone is going to treat her as I envision. Fortunately, Sydney was never the victim of true bullying. Over the years, there have been a handful of incidents where other people would pick on Sydney, but never anything that was truly an injustice. These matters were certainly dealt with quickly and aggressively, but the impetus of these situations was mere impetuousness and nothing too concerning. It goes without saying that there are other social struggles that Sydney faces.

It's hard to believe that there are people who can actually be mean to Sydney, but there are. But they do so in a passive way. At times, I think that can be worse than someone who does so in an active way. What I mean by passive is that it is what people don't do that hurts her. There have been many times where acquaintances, friends, and even family members leave Sydney out. Whether it is never returning her calls, not including her, or thinking that they can "get one over on her," and she realizes this. It hurts her, and it hurts me. If someone does not include her, it shows that she hasn't even crossed their minds, which can be very hard to swallow. There have been many days and nights where Sydney would be alone because of others' lack of inclusion, and it's hard to just accept. My family and I try to make others as aware of this as much as possible and always come to her defense, but we realize our biggest defense lies in prayer. We pray for others and their interactions with Sydney because God knows everything that is needed on both ends. We may think we know the solution, but God really does.

Bryan: What advice has she given you that has stuck with you?

CeeJay: Sydney's actions speak louder than her words. Her words are very powerful, but her actions really demonstrate how amazing she is. I see her struggle daily and watching her overcome every obstacle is inspiring. As a person with a disability, she has the world stacked against her. From a physical sense, the everyday actions that "normal" people take for granted are very difficult for her —tying her shoes, brushing her hair, etc. From a social sense, it is heartbreaking to know that she will not have the same experiences that everyone else has —wedding, engagement, job promotions, etc. To see her wake up with a smile on her face every single day puts everything in perspective. Sydney could easily dwell on the obstacles ahead of her and let it show, but she doesn't. Her outlook on life is everything, and everyone sees it.

Sydney also inspires me in her walk with God. At home, when we are getting ready for bed, oftentimes I will see her in her room alone reading her Bible, or on her knees praying. She does this every day, and it motivates me to want to be as knowledgeable about Jesus as she is. Her devotion to God certainly pays off because she has a connection with God like no other. Her prayer is powerful, very powerful. If anyone knows Sydney, they know how much her prayer means to them. People near and far reach out to Sydney when they need prayer, and that amazes me. Often, I am known as "Sydney's brother", and I like that. Because I'm known as "Sydney's brother" and not "CeeJay", it reminds me just how much of a difference my sister makes in others' lives, and that means the world to me. I'm proud to call her my sister and see just how special she is in every one of her interactions.

Bryan: How important is your walk with God to you?

156

CeeJay: My walk with God is everything to me. It is the foundation I was built on. God is the epicenter of my life and plays a role in every action I make. I'm so grateful to have been raised like this because I was instilled with roots. I was always told about roots and wings. My roots are the values and morals that I was raised with, and my wings give me the ability to go out and pursue my goals. I have always found that no matter how far I may stray away from God, I still have my roots, as I always come back to them and always will. God has gotten me through every point in my life, and I could not imagine what my life would be like without Him.

Sometimes, I look back on my accomplishments in awe. I wonder how I accomplished some of those goals, and I often contemplate that if I had to do it again, I don't know if I would be able to do it. But then I realize that God helped me achieve them. He gave me what I needed in order to get through each situation, He provided me with the strength to do so. I now know that I could not have done any of my accomplishments on my own, and I give all the glory to God. I'd be lost without God in my life. I pray every day constantly thanking God. Most times I don't even know what I'm thanking Him for. But I always thank Him for waking me up, for getting me through the day, for giving me exactly what I needed to get through a difficult situation, for His forgiveness, and for much more. I also pray that He helps me make the right decisions in everything I do. I understand that we are all sinners, but I try to always make the right choices even when I know I haven't always succeeded in the past. It comforts me to know that I am always forgiven. If I walked away from God today, I don't think I could live the same way. I don't understand how others live without God in their lives. To me, life would be pointless.

Bryan: What has been the biggest challenge you have faced but that God got you through?

CeeJay: My biggest challenge in life is change. When times get bad, I view change as something new, a fresh start. But when times are good, I hate change. Why would someone want to end something that is going so well? I think part of why I struggle with change is because most of the time it is out of my control. Whether that change may be leaving to go to a new school or having to say goodbye to a loved one, living with a new reality is very difficult at first for me. What reassures me is that I adapt, and God has helped me adapt. Sometimes when I reflect, I think about when times were good, and I can relive each and every moment. It oftentimes makes me sad because I know that I can never get those moments back no matter how hard I try. But God helps me take my past and turn them into memories that bring me happiness and joy when I think about them. He helps me change my thinking by viewing those moments as positives and focus on how great those times were and gives me hope to look toward the future that has great plans in store which is an optimistic outlook that memories are still ahead.

People change, too. It's hard to believe that one moment someone could think the world of you and the next they don't. But just as personality and thoughts change, so do others. When others change, your situation changes, and I don't like that. Many times, feelings change, and they are sometimes unexplainable. I am a people pleaser, and it's hard for me because as much as I try to be the person others want me to be, it still may not be enough. I realize that God made me who I am, and I cannot please everybody. I've learned to be my best self and focus on what I can control. I cannot control how others feel, so I choose not to worry about it.

Bryan: Do you have any advice for younger Christians?

CeeJay: My advice would be, don't worry. I think it is a good thing to be concerned about a lot of things because that keeps you on your toes. Being too comfortable is a bad thing and being aware is a key to success. But to constantly worry about everything is detrimental. One of my favorite excerpts from the Bible is Philippians 4, which instructs us not to worry. Don't worry about tomorrow because it is already taken care of; God is on our side.

When it comes down to it, worrying is pointless because every little thing is going to be okay. Even if the worst-case scenario happens, it's still going to be okay. I know that it's going to be okay because we have God with us. If we did not have God, then perhaps my piece of advice would be useless.

But because we have God to rely on, to get us through our difficulties, to lean on when we need Him, we will be okay. There is no situation that cannot be overcome or any circumstance that cannot be endured even in the most extreme cases. This does not mean that those times will not be tough, but with God's guiding hand, it is all possible. So, if we are going to be fine even if the worst happens, then there is nothing to worry about.

Bryan: In today's culture and especially in college, you are around many people, whether they be a different nationality, skin color, sexuality, gender, etc. How do you stand proud as a Christian but show compassion?

CeeJay: First, I treat everyone as equal. I like to acknowledge our differences, but more importantly, focus on our similarities. We are all equal, we are all children of God. I judge others by their character and who they are as a person, not by their physical attributes. I think that this is a very Christian way to think — to not let the color of one's skin or the sexuality of someone be the main priority when forming an opinion of them. For example, if I see that someone is being treated unfairly merely based on a physical characteristic, it angers me. On the other hand, if someone is getting flak for their poor showing of character, then I am more reluctant to show sympathy. I always try to be inclusive, to include those that are always left out, especially if it is because they are "different". Many times throughout my life I have seen others not be included. I know how it feels to be excluded, and I see firsthand how someone is excluded because of their disability — my sister. Having felt these emotions before and having seen others suffer from it, I always put my best foot forward to be aware of those who are excluded. Whenever the opportunity comes up, I make sure that I reach out to them and bring them along in whatever the scenario is.

Bryan: How have you used your Christian upbringing to guide your friends and yourself through the trials and tribulations in life?

CeeJay: I feel that one of my biggest strengths is helping others. I tend to prioritize loyalty, and it does not take much for me to be loyal to someone. Others claim that they are loyal, but when the going gets tough, they are nowhere to be found. The loyalty that my family and I believe in is different, and we would go to the ends of the Earth for others if that's what it takes. When others are in need of help, I view it as an opportunity for me to utilize my strengths. I feel that by helping others, I am not just showing my care and compassion for them, but I am showing them the work of God. All my help and advice revolves around God. For example, I've had friends and family deal with loss, depression, anxiety, and just general issues, and I always tell them about God, giving them sources of hope, inspiration, and happiness. There's a message from God in every possible scenario we can be in as humans, and it's up to us to find it and use it to our advantage. I feel that it is my calling to help others.

CeeJay is currently in his senior year at Villanova University.

Josh Swickard

Bryan: How did your dad being a pastor shape you, your behavior and how were you treated by your peers and the other parishioners in church?

Josh: Being a pastor's kid, or a PK, as it was called, I didn't realize that there was a negative connotation associated with it. I have three sisters, so there are four of us kids in my family. I was super fortunate and blessed to have parents that were very transparent, very honest, and very relaxed. None of us ever really rebelled or went against the grain. We never had a "Be home by 7 p.m.," or a "Footloose…dancing is a sin, childhood [*laughs*]."

I think what came with that was a lot of mutual respect and a friendship. Once we turned 18, there was a very clear, "You can call us for parental advice and we support you, but you're on your own." I respected that. Although, I hated it when I went broke in my early 20s.

Virtually everyone in my family works in the church and I am on a soap opera getting half-naked for a living [*laughs*]. There is a part of me that feels I could end up in ministry down the road.

I moved to Chicago after high school, and I started modeling. I remember I would work with people that would ask questions about me, and I would mention I was a pastor's kid, or a Christian. They would instantly get turned off by me. People would say something along the lines of, "Well, my whole life, Christians have been telling me I'm going to hell because of how I live."

But my understanding is that we had a ton of laws in the Old Testament and Jesus really honed in on Love God and Love People. In Matthew 26:39 it says, "Thou shalt love thy neighbor as thyself". I am so thankful that I do not have the right to say who is going to Heaven or hell. I also know that we are all beyond broken and are full of sin and in need of a savior.

Bryan: I think that gets lost on people who think they're being attacked for whatever the reason is, and that is not what church and Christianity is about. It is that everyone is broken and sins.

Josh: Absolutely. I think that is a challenge with the church that we've been facing. If we are not careful, we can come across as, "Well, I don't do this, I don't do that, and you do all those wrong things." That is why it can get such a negative view because I feel like there is so much judgment in the church.

Bryan: Did you ever feel a calling to be a pastor like your dad?

Josh: There are so many areas that I want to be like my dad and honestly, that is one of them. I don't know how it fits in the cards right now with everything I have going on. But I certainly don't shut the door on it. You know? If you write another book in 10 years and you have to track me down at a church in Central America, I would not be mad.

Bryan: When you started modeling and acting, was there any apprehension on you or your family's part, because of the reputation of the entertainment industry?

Josh: I am sure my parents were hesitant. What came with us turning 18 and them being like, "You do you," comes with good and bad. They didn't have a controlling, helicopter parent approach and with that, when your son says, "Hey, I want to go model. And this photographer said I should do Calvin Klein underwear modeling," you know, it's, suddenly like, "Whoa. Whoa, whoa, whoa [*laughs*]. What's going on?"

They would express their apprehension, but at the end of the day, they love me, want me to be wise, and want what's best for me. But I said it's something I wanted to do. I am sure they both were very nervous. I signed with a reputable agency. I talked my parents through it as I was learning it. I think my first job was for State Farm or something, standing outside of a college with a book bag.

Bryan: Have you ever been put in a position, whether it was modeling or acting, where you weren't comfortable with something for religious reasons, and did you speak up? If not, was there a fear that you would face consequences for standing up for your beliefs?

Josh: I mean, my first acting job was a Disney Channel show. Then I did a feel good rom-com. Now I am on a soap opera. On a soap opera, you get some stuff that is a hard pill to swallow as a Christian. As a husband it's different, and now as a father, it is even more different. To be honest, you could ask me this question today and the answer will be different than two years ago, and it will possibly be different two years from now. But in today's world, saying no to almost getting naked on TV will probably shut some doors, unfortunately.

It has been case by case for [wife] Lauren and me. It has now become, "How much creative control do we have on the racy days on set? Do we have a say in what we can and can't do?"

Bryan: Being on a soap opera and being a good-looking guy, they are going to want you to take your shirt off, show your physique and be in a romance all the time. Have you had to speak up and say, "Does Chase really need to be shirtless for this scene?"

Josh: Not really. *General Hospital* has been really courteous and respectful. They always send an email beforehand and ask, "Are you good with this? Are you not good with this?" Shirtless stuff, I don't really care too much about.

Bryan: Is that a fear because right now you are in the soap opera world or because *General Hospital* has been so respectful, you feel like they have your back as well?

Josh: Yes. I can't speak for any other shows than the one I am currently on, but there is definitely a mutual respect and a mutual understanding. I am very grateful for that.

Bryan: That is great because you do not want to place yourself in a situation that goes completely against your beliefs or makes you uncomfortable, just for a paycheck.

Josh: Lauren booked a role on a big movie that had a theatrical release, and it was a small role. She got to the table read and they completely changed the role. The script said, "As she steps in the room and takes off her top, and blah, blah, blah."

Lauren was like, "Whoa, whoa, whoa. Like, this isn't — " and the director was well-known and he's like, "Yeah, this is what it is now." And she's like, "Well, I'm not comfortable with it." And they recast her in a second.

Bryan: Your relationship with your grandfather is a beautiful thing. What has his impact been on your life?

Josh: Probably more than I will ever know. He is my mentor and, in a lot of ways, my best friend. But he is a master at bringing his faith into an everyday conversation. I've always looked up to him because he is just an anomaly of a person.

I don't think he would care about me telling you this, but he didn't get married until he was 34. He waited for his wife to become intimate. He has never been drunk. He has never smoked cigarettes, or weed, or anything. He was born in the mid '20s during the Great Depression, so some of this stuff wasn't even frowned upon. He just had this sense of not wanting dependencies in his life other than the Lord.

He really understood delayed gratification. He understood it at a really young age, you know, what does bring him joy. He will be 98, and he downhill skis, he does yoga, takes long walks, he bikes, he does Tai Chi.

Bryan: He is showing you up!

Josh: Yeah, he's oddly more active than I am. I thought that was always cool. I loved hearing about his life. He was on the frontlines in the 36th Infantry Division during World War II. He was missing in action and just has wild stories about going through that. I love hearing and talking about his stories.

When Covid hit, our show went dark, and he is in his late 90s, I figured his schedule looked like mine! I called him, and I said, "I would love to just pick a book of the Bible and you just dive in over FaceTime. We can do it a couple of days a week. No structure, no commitment. Why don't we start with the Gospels?" He suggested, "Awesome." It started maybe Monday, Tuesday, Wednesday and then it turned into every weekday. Throughout Covid, we were on FaceTime two to three hours in the morning almost every morning. I have a full journal, and then I switched to an iPad, and I have over 120 pages on it of him talking. I even recorded some of them.

I recommitted my life to the Lord. I saw a different kind of faith that I didn't have before. I can't speak for anyone else, but I feel like I've struggled with that Christian, "Yeah, I got that Sunday morning, pray before the meals," faith going on.

Watching grandpa do this daily, moment by moment relationship of, "God is your confidant, your everything, your best friend, your savior" and he is constantly talking to Him. I was like, "Whoa. This is different."

When a curveball is thrown his way, he smiles at it, and then his day somehow turns out better. I am seeing my grandfather live and I'm like, "Wait. Whatever you got, I want it."

My grandmother passed from Alzheimer's disease. Grandpa took care of her through all of that, and she died in a hospice bed in the living room. That man, the day she died, was sitting at the table in the kitchen just at a loss, feeling like a wreck, and it literally hit him. It hit him in that moment how much of what he was feeling and thinking was focused on him. "I'm so sad my wife died. Why me? Oh, God." He was putting this all on himself.

But then he flipped that thought process on its head and then just started thanking the Lord for the 60 years they had and for the Lord giving him that time with his wife Sue Brown for all those years, and the number of countries they visited, the cruises they went on, the amount of ballroom dancing hours they got under their belt. He replaced his grief with thanksgiving. Now he has a picture of her at his dining room table and they still eat every meal together. He looks at the photo and says, "I love you, Sue," often. And sometimes, when a good song comes on, he gets up and dances around the living room, just like he did with her.

Bryan: That is so sweet.

Josh: I mean, it's incredible. He just says it's all because of his faith, his relationship with the Lord. Watching him, part of me just feels like, I can do better than what I've been doing in the past. It starts with just loving people.

My grandfather and I were talking about marriage before I got married. He said, "One of the best things that your grandma and I did was we agreed to disagree. We didn't have to agree on anything or everything. We have our pillars in our lives that we agree on. And those are steadfast. But the tertiary stuff is not."

It's interesting, a lot of churches were -- let's say they're pro a certain president and they pray every day for them. But then a new president comes in and they don't pray for the new one anymore or vice versa. But, as a church, shouldn't we be falling on our faces for the previous, the current, and even our enemies.

Bryan: Not if you're a Christian it's not. We did a series at church based on *Emotionally Healthy Spirituality*, by Peter Scazzero. It deals with your family of origin and how they shape every aspect of your life. You had positive experiences with your grandparents, your parents, and now it is your and Lauren's turn with Savannah.

Josh: I was thinking about this. I was talking to my grandpa about this recently. One of his earliest memories was when he was living in a three-bedroom home with one bathroom off the kitchen in the 1930s. He was probably 8 and came down for breakfast and heard his dad in the bathroom. His dad was talking and so my grandfather put his ear up to the door and heard him saying, "Lord, you are so precious." From my grandpa saying that, and the prayers that shaped him, went into him, in generations prior to his, that he prayed, then becoming the ones he prayed over his kids, and the way the Lord works through them, all of those are going to radically affect Savannah. The decisions that I make as a man, as a Christian, as a dad, I am feeding into my great-grandchildren.

I have always believed that growing up in a good home provides way more positives than negatives. But there are undoubtedly negatives as well. One of those things was my parents never really yelled at each other, or if they did, it was behind closed doors. I can't say they didn't, but I never saw it. I remember the first time my wife and I got in a disagreement. I literally had this thought, "Oh, guess we can't be together," because I didn't think married people argued. There was this period of learning that this, obviously, is not true. In fact, you could argue, never disagreeing or arguing would be a bad sign, too. But since I did not see yelling growing up, I didn't have it in my toolbox to deal with it.

Lauren and I had a talk when we were engaged. We came to a decision together that we won't raise our voices at each other, ever, even if it is the gnarliest, most radical, horrible thing happening. We have only been together for five years, but so far, in all that time we have not yelled.

Bryan: Does that transfer to friendships as well or a boss yelling at you, or is it strictly with Lauren?

Josh: I have never even thought about it. My problem is I don't have many friends [*laughs*]. I'm a bit of a recluse. I have probably five good friends, and we don't care enough to yell, whatever the topic is.

I guess as an actor, you are kind of self-employed. But an executive producer, I guess, would be a boss at a show you are working on. I have been blessed with stellar bosses. Maybe if I did something that warranted yelling, I would probably deserve it [*laughs*].

Bryan: You and Lauren welcomed daughter Savannah last year. Who influenced you the most in how you want to parent her?

Josh: It is definitely my family's influence. That is such an integral part of why and who I am, that I almost don't know how to answer that, because I look at my grandpa, and my parents, and the marriages of each of my sisters, a lot of my daily choices of being a father or a husband play into that.

But lately, I just want to be present. For my daughter, what that looks like, even though she is still only a year and a half, they are things like not looking at my phone when she is with me and trying to look her in the eyes.

I love holding her, hugging her, and laughing with her. She is already the smiliest little girl. We think it's because anytime Lauren and I see her, we'll literally go, "Savannah!!!" It's like I have come back from being away for weeks or something every time I see her.

So, with Lauren, it may be before she is awake, I bring her coffee, and put it next to her side of the bed, or if we're watching a show, I will rub her feet, or cook. I try to do as much cooking as I can. Not sure I can do enough to thank my wife for what she went through giving birth.

For me, I've always struggled with trying to be Christ-like rather than just talking about Him. What would He do in this situation?" In a lot of the New Testament, you saw that He washed feet. He served people. If you were interviewing my daughter, when she's 18 and has just left the house, and you asked, "What was your dad like," I would love for the first thing out of her mouth to be, "Man, he has a servant's heart. The guy loves to serve."

But with that said, we are all human. My brain is still very human. So, when she cries at 2 a.m., I'm thinking, "Gosh dang-it," and then I try to go in with a smile or, you know, if Lauren says something cross, and suddenly, it's like, "I don't want to cook you a meal anymore" [*laughs*]. We are all human.

I think it is all about open communication. When we first got married, if we ever had a hard talk, and this sounds silly, but we would pray about it before we get into the conversation. It would be something as simple as, "Lord, you know our hearts. You know we love each other and that we ask You to be in this conversation. Amen."

Bryan: Were you like-minded when you got together in terms of spirituality?

Josh: Yeah. I mean, she didn't grow up a pastor's kid, but she went to a Christian school. She loved her Apologetics class. I still have one of the first notes she wrote me, a couple weeks into us meeting.

She said she thought the reason we bonded was because of my faith. She enjoyed being around that. And I agree, we definitely bonded over our faith. I don't know how successful our marriage would be if we didn't have it.

Bryan: How have you used your platform to encourage others to dig deeper into a love for Christ and have you met resistance in doing so? Or do you try to fly under the radar?

Josh: That's a hard question for me because I am still figuring it out, as a Christian, as an actor, as a husband, father, of how transparent to be. With social media I am in both camps. Your social media is for promoting your projects and work, but it is also to give a little glimpse into your family and what we are about with our faith.

I have felt convicted so many times that I could be better at doing more social media-driven posts to create the conversation of cultivating that atmosphere of faith-based content. The resistance I have met is the evil one in the back of my head and not so much fans being like, "Why are you believing in God?"

I think my fan base is so kind and cool, and I appreciate them so much. I think they know who I am, and they know what I am about. I think if I was more open about my faith, the fans would think it's rad.

Bryan: What is the best advice a family member has given you about staying true to your faith, and what advice do you have for those who might be afraid to be open about their own religious and spiritual lives?

Josh: Get a daily routine in place. To this day still, I feel so much further from the Lord when I'm not diving into the Word. It doesn't have to be cracking open a Bible. It could be reading a devotional or the opening *The Bible* app, which has amazing devotionals. They take seconds. I think I get so, "I have to read a chapter a day," or "a book a day," or "the whole Bible in a year," or nothing. There is no in-between.

Bryan: Fellowship is very important. I'm in a men's group at church and it is a true Christian brotherhood. We all have our own lives, but when we are in that room, it's about supporting and empowering each other. We pray for and over each other.

Josh: I love 1 Corinthians 16:13-14. "Be on your guard. Stand firm in the faith. Be men of courage. Be strong. And do everything in love." When my grandfather and I started our Bible studying during Covid, the first thing he asked was, "What is your life verse?" I didn't have one. I scoured the Bible, and I came upon that. And he was like, "Oh, that's a good one." I say that in the shower each morning.

I remember sitting in the back of my mom's minivan on a road trip, asking God to come into my heart, and did that at least once a month in case the last time did not count [*laughs*]. I was just looking outside at the stars, and I had my face pressed up against the cold glass and just started crying. I was probably 11, but I just felt close to the Lord. I can't even explain what it was. There was just this overwhelming sense that God is good.

I love music. Both my parents were music performance majors, and it was very integral in our lives. Sometimes a worship song will hit just right. I will be driving in my car, and I have to pull over for a second.

Growing up, my grandparents had a small little lake house in Wisconsin. When we stayed there, every morning we would come down for breakfast and we would pray. But then after we would pray, they would always sing one or two hymns.

Bryan: What advice would you give someone who is nervous to share their faith with others?

Josh: The first thing I would say is that's okay to be nervous. I am a pastor's kid who was crawling through the pews. I am 30 and I am still nervous. I don't think being nervous is a bad thing at all. I think that makes you human. More often than not, I've gone into a conversation, or a post, or whatever, and been like, "Man, I'm nervous."

Find a friend who can be an accountability partner. The number of times I have called a friend and said, "Hey, I feel far from the Lord. Will you do this five-day devotional with me?" and we talk about it every night. Hopefully, you have friends in your lives that are cool with that. If not, find a church. Find a small group. Get connected.

Josh currently stars as Chase on the ABC soap opera General Hospital. He and his wife, Lauren, reside in California where they are raising their daughter, Savannah. Instagram: @joshswickard

Jordi and Kaitlin Vilasuso

Bryan: What was your relationship with God like growing up?

Jordi: I grew up Catholic. I was baptized and my parents sent me to a Catholic school called Epiphany School, which is a well-known Catholic school in South Miami. I went to it for 10 years. I would say, spiritually and religiously, I did have a very strong relationship with God from the beginning.

My parents constantly had a lot of iconography around the house: crosses, beautiful paintings of Mary, stuff like that. My grandmother on my dad's side was very religious. She lost her husband the year before I was born and never remarried and lived with her daughter, my dad's sister. I always remember there being a strong relationship with God from her. She mourned her husband for, like, 25 years, until she passed.

I do distinctly remember what helped propel my relationship. There was a priest by the name of Father Michael, and he was a younger priest at my church. Catholic church can be, for the lack of a better word, boring, especially for an 11-year-old who is mischievous and trying to get into all sorts of things.

But this guy had a very charismatic way of delivering the homily that spoke to all the people at the church, and I was a huge fan. From there, I would go out of my way to talk to him, and he was very encouraging.

I had religion as one of the classes in my Catholic school. He would guide us through a Christian meditation, which I thought was one of the coolest experiences growing up. It has really served me throughout my life, and I just love starting my day like that. I just see God working in my life while doing it.

Kaitlin: For me, it was a little different, but a little similar, in the sense that my parents were amazing at making sure that I formed that foundation. I went to a beautiful little Christian school in Fort Lauderdale, Christ Church, and it was amazing. I went there for elementary school and middle school, and then high school I went to Westminster Christian School, which was a Presbyterian school. It was a little strict.

My parents went to a nondenominational church, so we went to Calvary Chapel Fort Lauderdale, where I fell in love with Christian music. For me, during all the ups and downs, I feel like Christian music always took me back to my relationship with Jesus. I am very fortunate, in the sense that my parents instilled that in us, and I've known Jesus from such a young age, and that has never left me. I am so grateful for that.

When Jordi and I started dating, I gave him a little booklet with all these Christian songs and lyrics that I loved and how they had taken me through difficult times. I feel like Christian music, for me, is prayer, in a sense. I think ever since then, our faith has kind of just grown together. But God has had His hand on our relationship since the beginning. I have known Jordi since I was 17.

Jordi: You knew of me way before, but we met when you were 17!

Kaitlin: I grew up watching Jordi on *Guiding Light*. My family would watch all the CBS shows. My grandmother did, my mom did, and then obviously I did. I used to run home from school in high school to watch Jordi as Tony Santos on *Guiding Light*. And I loved him.

It just so happened that Jordi and I had the same manager because I was acting. This manager knew that I had a crush on him, whatever. I was in Los Angeles for the premiere of *Monster*, which is a movie that I had done way back in the day. She asked if I wanted to meet Jordi, which I did. We went to the Broadway Deli with my mom and the manager. We had lunch, and then we ended up going on a date. And then I went back to Florida, I finished high school, and ended up going to college. Over the years Jordi and I, our paths would cross, and sometimes we were just friends if I was dating somebody, or if he was dating somebody.

Other times, there was a romantic element to it, but we never seriously dated until I was 23. I had really tried to make an acting career work in New York, and it was just not happening. I was working three jobs and I still couldn't pay my rent. My mom and my sister were in Los Angeles., and my mom was like, "Pack up your stuff, come live with us."

I did, and I remember I was with them one night, and I said to my mom, "I'm so lonely." I wrote to Jordi on Facebook, and we still have the message. It was just so beautiful, the timing of it. I was in a long-term relationship, on and off, from, like, 15 to 22. I constantly think, had I not gone through that relationship, and the turmoil of it, I don't know that I would have appreciated Jordi and all of his qualities.

If you look back just over both of our lives, it just all makes so much sense how we are here today together. Fast-forward three years later, Jordi's asking me if I'm ready to get married. I had moved to Los Angeles to act, and I wasn't acting. I was apprehensive about getting married when I did not know what my future looked like career-wise.

But, also, I think there was something in me that I wasn't 100 percent sure about. I started praying for clarity and direction, and I've never prayed for anything so intently in my life. Two weeks later, Easter morning, we found out that we were pregnant with Riley. And I was like, "Hey, whenever you're ready. I'm ready now [*laughs*]."

We went to mass that evening with his parents. The entire homily was about how Jesus loved the children and always brought children to him.

Bryan: Jordi, you have been open about how you had a lot of growing up to do while you were starting out in the industry. How did God help you with that?

Jordi: A lot. I think God saved me from a lot of stuff that would have possibly created obstacles to Kaitlin and I getting together. I didn't have a lot of men in my life to mentor me about relationships and marriage.

I've talked to other men about this as well, shared that it was this very shallow way of living. Having multiple relationships was a sense of achievement, whether you had relationships with other women, you were acting out, or you were just living this shallow lifestyle.

I knew, for whatever reason, that Katie and I had something very special from the beginning. When she gave me the -- I'm tearing up -- when she gave me the journal with the Christian lyrics, I was completely sold because that spoke to me. I knew that, with Katie, with our foundation, we will get through anything. I felt that innately. We have been together 10 years.

Kaitlin: I think, as Jordi has grown as a man in Christ, we have started to realize that that is a part of his story, and he can impact other young men by telling them, "Hey, I did this, and this is why it didn't serve me, and this is why it's not going to serve you." Had he not done all of that, would he have this testimony that he does? He has an amazing group of men that he spent time within a program called Unravel. I think that's when he really discovered that your past wasn't just your past. But there's so much to be gained from that. All these mistakes, all these things that he went through that he is not proud of, does serve others.

Jordi: After I graduated high school, my father had sent me to a retreat called Emmaus with a much older group of men. In the Gospel of Luke, it tells of one of the early appearances of Jesus after his crucifixion and the discovery of the empty tomb on the road to Emmaus. This group I was a part of was comprised of men who were all older than me, by at least 10 years. They were getting into the nitty-gritty of life and being very honest and very transparent about what they were going through. That had a huge impact on me, in terms of the humanity of it all.

Whether it was casual sexual interactions, struggling with pornography, the way that they looked at women, or even how their minds thought about what a woman was supposed to provide for him. There was a lot of machismo and bravado in Miami when I was growing up. I was working out and I was jacked, but it's all such bullshit at the end of the day.

Bryan: What I love about you guys is that your podcast, *Making It Work*, is very open and honest. You do not shy away from difficult topics or showing emotion. How important is that to both of you that your listeners get the authentic versions of you?

Jordi: I think it's important, especially with mental health, whether it's on our podcast, or just looking at the landscape of our society right now, in terms of school shootings, the isolation that a lot of people have been through because of Covid and feeling alone. We wanted to be as real as possible, while also not being afraid to share our thoughts. So many things can be taken out of context, for whatever reason. Whether we're speaking about the tragedy in Uvalde, and then trying to stay out of it from any political point of view.

Kaitlin: We originally decided to do the podcast because we have been open about our struggles and because we're super-passionate about marriage. I am a child of divorce. My parents are amazing parents, but they were not good together, and I saw a lot of things growing up. My dad has one of most beautiful faiths that you could ever imagine, and my mom, as well.

But together it didn't work. In terms of a relationship, I grew up not knowing that you could have a relationship that was not like theirs, to be honest. When Jordi and I got married, it was very clear that I had such a different perspective of marriage because he had only seen happy marriages. His parents have a beautiful marriage that was filled with challenges that they worked through.

Jordi: My parents separated when I was 24. I was all for it because I wanted the fighting to stop. I wanted to stop picking teams. My sister, unfortunately, had to put herself in rehab during that time, which was one of the silver linings of them being separated.

But there were all these things, all these foundations falling apart. The marriage, my family, my sister being in that dynamic because she was the youngest one. But then I remember going to my dad and being like, "Dad, why don't you just leave Mom? Just go?" We had this very candid conversation. He's like, "You know what, Jordi? I can't see myself with another woman, I can't see myself dating. For better or worse, I love your mom." They did the hard work and reconciled and maybe they didn't realize it at the time, but that really struck a chord with me.

Kaitlin: We found out about being pregnant with Riley on Easter, we got engaged on Mother's Day, got married in August, and then had Riley in November. There was a lot going on. Right after our wedding Jordi's dad was diagnosed with Mantle Cell lymphoma, which was very aggressive, but thank God, caught at Stage 1.

Jordi was on *All My Children* at the time, which had just gotten cancelled. We were living in Los Angeles, and he looked at me and said, "Why don't we just move back home? I can be there for my dad, and we're going have this baby."

We packed up and moved back to Fort Lauderdale, and we found ourselves living in my mom's house. Riley was about six months old, and I started having these thoughts, "You know, all I've ever known is, eventually, he's going to cheat on me, anyways, right? So why don't we just call it what it is? We've got a beautiful baby, we both love her, and, you know, it just, it is what it is, and let's just end it before it gets ugly."

I really thought that was the mature and the logical thing to do. Jordi was not having it and found a therapist for us right up the street from my mom's and we started going to therapy. We were very fortunate because Julia has been in our life for nine years and she's incredible at what she does. She has an amazing knack for letting him say something, then me saying something, and then cuts through all of it, knows what the problem is, and how to fix it. She has really been a blessing.

Bryan: What are the things on your walk that really have served both of you in terms of leaning-in on God separately, and then bringing that to the marriage to keep moving forward?

Jordi: Currently I am in the season where I am leaning heavily into my relationship with God. The actor's life can really be a testimony to faith because you don't know what is going to happen in terms of a job. Some of the greatest experiences and things that I can lean on in my own journey was when I saw God's hand at work. It was so distinct, all the things that happened, how God was there with us and took care of us.

After being let go from my last steady gig on the soap opera *The Young and the Restless,* our dear friend, Marni, invited us to church. Katie, and our daughters Riley and Everly, and I hadn't been to church because of the pandemic, but we'd watch it on TV/online. The pastor that was there, his message, was all about how as a Christian, God gives you these things to endure: suffering, sacrifices, challenges, to build your faith.

It was everything that I had to hear, and it literally felt like God's hand was grabbing my heart and squeezing it, and looking me in the eye and saying, "Are you listening to this? Are you hearing what is being said right now?" I was bawling in my chair. He just shook me, and I loved that.

I have made it a point to also lean into the Christian disciplines, meditation, fasting, worship, prayer, all these things that I learned through my men's group.

I have been able to be vulnerable with Kaitlin, where it's like, "Babe, I'm having a tough time today, can we just pray together?" I feel so much safer with this environment of faith, and God's love surrounding us, that I'm able to share those things in a vulnerable way to her that can be raw and upsetting, but it helps us get through it in a better way.

Bryan: Kaitlin, do you handle things the same way as Jordi?

Kaitlin: I think it's easier for me to lay it all out on the table. I don't know if that's just because I'm a female. Jordi has the thoughts of masculinity, and being a provider, and all these things, and showing weakness.

I think it takes him humbling himself, for sure. James 4:10 says, "Humble yourself in the eyes of the Lord." Me, I am just like, "Man, I'm a mess, I'm having a hard time today [*laughs*]." That's a little bit easier for me. But with everything that Jordi was just saying, I feel like it's such a reminder that, if you seek God, He is there. All we have to do is seek Him.

Sometimes I am a little bit stubborn with that. My walk has changed so much because of him. Perhaps that's because I'm not a very disciplined person. The discipline that he has, I see. I see how it's grown his faith so much, and that's really touched me.

God's plan has always been better than our plan. Had I been in control of this life of mine, we would not have what we have today. There is a certain amount of peace in that. Sometimes he needs that reminder, and sometimes I need that reminder.

Jordi: It is funny how the relationship works, too. Because there are a lot of times where I'm just like, "Oh, my God, how am I even going tell her this? I don't want to bring her down," and she's the opposite: She's bringing me up, she's coming from this place of strength. And I'm like, "Where the heck did that come from?"

Kaitlin: I don't know. I feel that marriage is beautiful like that, and God is beautiful like that.

When I miscarried, it was such a huge part of our marriage, because it was a huge bump in the road. When I found out I was pregnant with our third, I wanted another baby, and Jordi was on the fence, but not really feeling it. When we found out I was pregnant, I was definitely more excited than he was. And then when I realized that there were problems with the pregnancy, there was definitely a sort of desperation, where if this pregnancy didn't work, that was the end of us having more babies.

And when I did miscarry, I felt like I was grieving something alone and that we should be grieving together. I think there's an element of that that happens regardless, for women. Because obviously you're going to feel more connected.

I never expected him to feel what I felt, but it hit me even differently just because we weren't on the same page about having a third child. It took close to a year for every argument to not end up being about the miscarriage.

It was on my birthday that things really hit the fan. We were not in a good place. I remember we were having people over for my birthday, and on my birthday the year before, we had told all our friends that I was pregnant. There were so many emotions coming back. And I was like, "I can't do this." I was in the bathroom on the floor because that's where every mom goes when she needs to cry! I was on the floor, and he came in. I was having a panic attack and he just held me. For me, it was the first time that I felt like he really got it. Like, that he saw me, and how it had impacted me. I think therapy really helped us. There are these things that you go through in a marriage and in life, that the only thing that is going to keep you together is God, at the end of the day.

Bryan: Was your miscarriage your strongest moment of, "Why, God?"

Kaitlin: I think, for me, yes, but not for him. A friend of mine who miscarried a few times and had a crazy fertility journey, wrote me right after the miscarriage and she said, "I will always consider you a mom of three." It broke my heart because I didn't want to consider myself a mom of three. I think I tried to run from that pain as much as I could.

180

There are just so many questions that come out that it took me a long time to be at peace with it. And the reality was Jordi and I needed to get on the same page.

Bryan: Jordi, what was your biggest questioning-of-God moment, of whether He was there for you or not?

Jordi: God's timing can be hard. But I do see God working through a lot of tragedies. Our relationship is deeper because of whatever we've been through, what we have been able to endure. Sometimes you just have to humble yourself and say, "I don't have the answers, but I submit myself to you and I trust in your word and in your work."

Bryan: How have you navigated being in an industry where being a Christian is not always looked at favorably?

Jordi: I think you have to be intentional, it's not something that comes easy in Los Angeles.

Kaitlin: In Hollywood, Christians can be seen as judgmental. The last thing I would want to come off as is judgmental. I feel like we hold it close, but I think if anybody knows us at all, I would hope that there's some underlying element to the fact that we know God. I think, also, what we put out on social media makes it clear to people that we're Christians.

Bryan: In general, it is also a tricky time to be raising children today and what is being taught in schools.

Kaitlin: I feel like I've kind of taken the reins on that. I've made myself be very aware of exactly what is being taught. Because they are, instead of just teaching like teachers used to teach, there is an underlying ideology being taught. Our kids are in public school in California. I will tell Jordi things that I'm concerned about, and we'll talk through them, and then we'll talk about how we're going to speak to the kids about it.

Because we do always want to teach them to love and accept: "And this is how Jesus was, and this what Jesus has called us to do." But at the same time these are our values, and a lot of the things that are being taught are just not good for these kids' mental health at the end of the day.

Take Christianity or religion out of the equation and just from a mental health perspective, it doesn't serve them to think that they're responsible for the sins of people before them. Or to question themselves physically with things that they're not capable of understanding. It is unfortunate that we're having to have those conversations.

Our daughter, Riley is nine, and she's in fourth grade. Our other daughter, Everly, is going into first grade next year, so we've got a little bit more time with her. But, with Riley, we've definitely had to address things when she gets home.

Jordi and I'll sit down with her and be like, "Hey, this is something that's being taught right now because there's a lot of tension, and this person feels that way and that person feels this way. But, as a family, you know, this is what we feel like. We try to take it back to the Bible and to biblical principles, while also being accepting and loving toward others.

Jordi: Growing up, my father always made our home a very open place to discuss things. I want my girls to not look at me as this overbearing father who doesn't want them dating or controlling them. I want them to be able to be like, "Hey, listen, I like this boy," and I want to be loving and encouraging, but also enforce the ideas of respect, and point out the things that they can take away from their mother.

But I want them to feel like, they can always come to us. I want them to know that it's a safe space, nothing's taboo, we're not going judge them for talking to us about things. We want to educate them. And the only way that that's going to happen in our household amid what's being taught in California in the public schools, is if we're just like, "Hey, listen, we'll talk this through, we'll educate you, we'll give you wisdom. And then, hopefully, that gives you the strength to understand these things from our Christian perspective."

Kaitlin: I just want to let them be little as long as I can. Thank God, Jordi has been such an active father in all of this. Because if it was up to me, I think I'd keep them in a bit of a bubble, for sure.

Something that we've done from the very beginning with the girls is prayers every night before bed; things that we're praying for, people that we're praying for. Then we'll do "The Lord's Prayer" and then we'll do a prayer that Jordi grew up saying, which is in Spanish.

Jordi: It's a guardian angel prayer, called, *Angel de mi Guardia*. I want them to see that I have a relationship with God because that is important. Riley, she's very curious. Katie got her a Bible for Valentine's Day, which is really sweet. Both of our daughters have beautiful hearts. We're very blessed in that way. Christian music is usually playing as the soundtrack in our homes or in our cars. We really lean into that.

Kaitlin: Our marriage is a testament to our faith, as well. I think we've made it very clear that Mommy and Daddy are not perfect, but we made a promise to God, and we will preserve the family that we're so blessed with. Riley will ask all the time, whenever she hears about friends' parents getting divorced, she'll be like, "Oh, you and Daddy are ... that's not going happen to us, right?" It's like, "No, baby. We made a vow to God." I feel like they know that we have that foundation in our marriage, which hopefully will impact them growing up.

Jordi is a Daytime Emmy Award-winning actor who has worked in the entertainment industry for over two decades. The Vilasusos host a podcast, Making It Work which can be found here: podcasts.apple.com/us/podcast/making-it-work/. The couple currently reside in California and are the parents to daughters Riley and Everly. Instagram: @jordivilasuso @kaitlinvilasuso @makingitwork

Cody Anthony

Bryan: When you were growing up, were you part of a denominational or nondenominational church?

Cody: I grew up Catholic. It was partially structured for a while there. It was kind of hit or miss because we would go as kids and then my parents got divorced when I was three years old.

So, I know we went up until I was three. Then I went to Catholic school, which is very structured. I went back in the day when you got slapped on the wrist with a ruler. Middle school was a little less structured because my mom was figuring out her walk. She wasn't pushing this strict Catholic church idealism very much.

We would go to Christian churches and Catholic churches, but we ended up at the Catholic church my eighth-grade year. I loved that church because they were kind of pioneering the young teen mass. They would literally call it "Teen Mass" on Sunday. It was at 6:30 at night and it was a great experience. The Catholic church before that, I didn't have a great experience and I didn't really have a connection.

I did not understand doing the Hail Mary and a lot of the prayers. I really didn't understand mass at all because I just felt like they were speaking in tongues because it was so strictly out of the Bible. I think for a young man or a young kid, that communication needs to be clearer in order to understand how to create a relationship.

We stayed at that church all the way through my sophomore or junior year of high school and then I sort of strayed. I had a lot going on and there was a lot of family stuff going on. It was just kind of a mess toward the end of high school, and I was getting ready to move to Los Angeles.

I just had not found my relationship again as a young adult. It took a couple of years for me to start to understand that. I always sought it, but I think I had some church hurt from the beginning that I had to deal with.

Bryan: When you moved out to Hollywood, were you worried that the relationship that you had started to build would go by the wayside because of the industry you were going to pursue?

Cody: No, I don't think I was worried about that because I was so strong-minded. I was out there to do one thing and that was to work hard and stay focused. The beginning of my career, I was obsessed with staying focused on my acting and being in acting schools, my courses, and learning and understanding the craft.

I wasn't worried about it. I was still finding it. I still had my conversation and my relationship with Him. Even today, you are just always seeking a stronger relationship and a stronger connection with Him. But I didn't know or have anybody out there, so I definitely leaned on Him quite a bit.

I didn't find a church until probably three years into being out there. I found Mosaic Church, which is led by Erwin McManus. When he got up and spoke, I was like, "This guy's incredible." The way he communicates is just insane.

That is when I really started connecting. I think I was 19 or 20. That is when my walk out there really started to be strong, because I found a place to worship, to connect with people and be in the house of God.

I did a big Christian film that really matured me and my faith and showed me a whole different world that I didn't know existed. It was called *Not Today*, which was filmed in India. I felt my walk was strong and that's one of the reasons I wanted to tell the story. *Not Today* was about human trafficking and child trafficking.

We filmed and lived in India for almost six months, and we got thrown right into it. The director [Jon Van Dyke] was very, very adamant about not building any sets. We were shooting this guerilla-style in the slums to show how it really is.

We sat down and interviewed these people who had survived being kidnapped and put through the hell that they got put through with human trafficking. It is crazy seeing how these people live, but also the joy that they still have in their heart.

We would bring them crayons and chalkboards and the kids were so happy and content. It made me think about how I have always been very financially driven. I have expensive taste. I'm not going to lie about it. I enjoyed making money, and I was very driven in that sense.

Growing up, it was innate; it was taught to me that that's what brought happiness. I had a person in my life and that's all he lived for: money. When I saw these people living in tents and cooking rice in the pot and they were just incredibly happy, I was like, "Okay, that's what being rich is all about." Because they had their family and they had people that they loved and cared about. They didn't know anything different. Or maybe they did, but they were content and happy. That whole trip just really grounded me and changed my life because I had done *Fame* and I had just done *Bring It On*.

I was starting to get a lot of momentum, a lot of fluffy press and my career started blowing up a little bit. Then I went and did *Not Today* and left for a long time. It was the right choice for me to do. I'm really picky about projects. That enhanced my walk for sure.

Bryan: While you were out there in L.A., you met your wife, Stephanie. She came from a solid foundation with God and the church, right?

Cody: Yeah, she did. She was very lucky to have two wonderful parents that were very strong in their faith. They went to Bible college and everything. Her mom is very anointed, so that was a huge part of her life forever. She had a very healthy relationship with God.

It shows today because she's the type that does not have to be in church every Sunday and her relationship is so strong. For me, I need to be in the house of God, I need to be in worship, I need to feel it. Stephanie has such a strong foundation with her relationship and that's really carried us through some hard times in our marriage and during hard times that I've been through. She's a solid one. And she's been my rock for a long time.

Bryan: When you were dating, did you guys attend church together while also navigating being a young couple in Hollywood?

Cody: Yes, our foundation was set on going to church together. When we met it was just one lunch and she went back to Nashville. I stayed in L.A. for another four months. All we could do was sit on Skype at the time. We would talk and then on Sundays and Wednesdays, we would stream church together. We would stream Mosaic, actually.

That set the most important foundation that I've ever had in a relationship. That set the foundation to where we, obviously, can get through anything. We are a team, and we push through together. We know where each other's hearts are.

In our long-distance relationship, we set the foundation of faith and made sure that we were equally yoked. I will put everything on that being why we have been able to have our marriage last eight years and to last forevermore, is the foundation because of the church we would watch twice a week together.

Bryan: How has that foundation affected how you and Stephanie are raising your three beautiful kids, Lyla, Elijah, and Noah.

Cody: It's very important for us that they find their own walk. Especially since for me, there are a lot of things that were forced in my life that I ended up rebelling against. That goes all the way from sports to church to how they want to dress. We encourage and we set an example through prayers at night. Obviously, they love going to church on Sundays because our church here, LifePoint, has a great children's program. The kids have fun, and they learn a lot. They talk about Jesus a lot. They look at the moon, they point up, and Elijah will be like, "Dad, Jesus." That's always cool.

I think as parents, we have to lead by example, show that our walk is so strong, and encourage because God's not supposed to be used as a weapon. We never want to even walk close to that line. I think the most important thing for us is that they see what we are doing and that they see when we pray. They see it in the way we treat people. They see us worshiping and throwing our hands up and they do the same thing. They will find their walk and when they do, I will sit down and have talks for hours about it when they're mature enough to understand what that connection feels like. But they are still pretty young. I think just leading by example and just doing what we do, I think they'll be encouraged to find their walk and show how much happiness it brings.

Bryan: I know that you have gone through some really rough patches in your life from your early childhood, right up until recently. Walk the readers through what you're comfortable sharing and how God has been with you every step of the way lifting you higher.

Cody: First, I've had a lot of really great things happen to me in life, a lot of positive things. I've gotten to work, be around and be a part of a really exciting community in the entertainment business. But it's a very vulnerable place to be when you're at that level.

There are a lot of evil people around in this world. When you are in the public eye, people can write or say anything that they want about you, and they will. I am not very good with that yet. I struggle from anxiety quite a bit. I always have since I was a kid.

I grew up partially in an abusive household, mentally and physically, because of my parents' divorce. I just went through a lot as a kid that gave me a lot of fear and anxiety that I carried with me into adulthood. I have definitely been through a lot, but I'm stronger because of it. It has shown me how strong I really am and how my mom led by example, with what she went through as well, and never gave up. That has carried me through a lot of the hard times from when I was a young kid until recently.

You have to trust God and just keep moving forward. I carried a lot of pain from my childhood up until recently. I see a psychologist and I am in therapy. It is a hard thing to get rid of when you have a lot of anger in you, when somebody has done you wrong, or some stuff that has been done to you is very unfair.

You just have to trust your gut. That's one thing that I just didn't do. I didn't listen to my closest people around me. And it ended up biting me in the ass. If anything, I learned to trust my gut once again. Just because the relationship's supposed to be there from a child to a parent, doesn't mean that I should be.

When you're treated wrong, it's okay to let go. Blood doesn't always make family. When you have wonderful people around you, having the same bad feeling and just saying, "you have to let this person go," because they just feel like someone's going to take advantage or do you wrong. You have to listen to those peers.

If I learned one thing from my mom, who's a wonderful lady, who I love so much, and my sister, too, is that you have to battle through and do what is right. The forgiving parts have been really hard for me. Like I said, I've held on to a lot of that anger until recently.

It took a lot of work, a lot of talking, a lot of therapy and a lot of recognizing where those hurts are at, digging through my brain because my anxiety, my confusion and anger, would get so bad that I would just want to sleep. You get yourself into a depression and it got bad for me. It got to a point where it was too much for me to handle and I just wanted to sleep. I don't think I was ever suicidal because I would never do that to my mother, my sister, to Steph or the babies. But my coping mechanism was just trying to go to sleep, and that is depression.

It is just really wild because these moments where things are going really well and then all of a sudden, you detach yourself from your walk, from God, or just don't feel as connected, it's not a priority in the moment, and sometimes it's a way that I'll never understand. Some people might relate to that, and I think it is to bring you back on your knees and get you in that prayer position.

It seems to me that whenever I lose that walk or that priority of that connection, He has gotten a way to dramatically bring me back to Him. Even through all I have been through, I have never gotten mad at God. I just never had that in me. It's just brought me back to prayer every single time that I go through anything. I know that calling is big. I know my relationship with and my connection to God is very strong. God wants me to fulfill that purpose and be able to strengthen others by the stuff that I've been through.

Bryan: You and I bonded years ago after our first meeting and we didn't really know too much about each other. We formed a Christian brotherhood that will not break. How important is that for you to have other Christian brothers to walk alongside you and that you walk alongside?

Cody: It is so important. It's funny; I was thinking about that today. I have learned the importance of who you surround yourself with. I've learned the importance of the relationship with God that your friends have.

I think that you need to surround yourself with people that you admire, but also might admire you in the same way, respect you and treat you with that respect. Yet I think that that's the most important thing, especially as a man, to have friends that are on the walk as well, that are faithful and that are focused.

I think if you have three or four friends that are insanely close to God and in a relationship, you're only going to get stronger, and you are going to be the next one that's just like them. I think the importance of surrounding yourself with the right people is one of the biggest lessons I've ever learned in my life, so that is one of my top priorities of who we keep in our lives. Same with Steph and who we spend time with as a couple.

Bryan: In the book I talk about how I had a supernatural occurrence during a medical emergency, through the prayer of a close mentor. When you were going through your most recent struggle, I prayed over you and also wanted the immediate response that I received, and when that didn't happen, I felt like I had failed you, which is not how that works.

Cody: I know I've got a lot of prayer warriors in my corner. The power of prayer is absolutely mind-boggling and insanely beautiful to me. It's real. I've had a couple of experiences with it. But the power of prayer, it works. I posted something the other day on my Instagram, a lot of people say, "Oh, hey, I'll pray for you." That does not always have to be said because if you are really praying for them, they are going to know it, they are going to feel it and they are going to get through things.

The amount of prayer that I have in my corner is some pretty powerful stuff and I am so grateful for it. The experience of prayer has changed my life and has gotten me through some really hard times, while also giving me great times.

People are praying for me to have a healthy and happy family. I am so blessed to have a beautiful wife and three incredible kids that are all just healthy, beautiful, sweet kids with personality plus. The power of prayer is kind of magical.

Bryan: Speaking of Stephanie and the kids, you are all about to embark on a new life in Texas. It is wonderful for you guys to get a fresh start. Have you found a church out there and are you nervous taking such a huge step?

Cody: We have been doing some research. I found a church called Austin Stone Community Church that we are going to check out. We are going to go out and explore. I am very relationship-driven. I've been lucky to have great relationships with all my pastors. We are going to get involved and start serving and see where we connect the most.

I am not stressed about that whatsoever. I know we are going find a great home church. I will miss my church and my pastor here terribly. But we are so excited for the new house and the new adventure. It's a family move; we are moving to another state and are going to be starting over in a brand-new place.

I thrive in new cities. Stephanie is very excited. She's ready to go. She's been in Nashville for 20 years now. It excites me to see how excited she is and how excited the kids are. It is a beautiful thing, and we are very lucky to be able to go and comfortably move. We found a great house out there the kids are going love. It is one of the most exciting times in my life, for sure.

Bryan: You mentioned the importance of the relationship with your pastors. I know I have said it a million times, but do you see yourself being called to lead in a pastoral role and walking alongside someone on their walk in that capacity?

Cody: I have worked as a pastor for a short time, and it was great. I loved it. I feel like it is part of my purpose to use my experiences to bring people to Him. I really do. My thing is, I want to feel a thousand percent about my walk and my relationship for a very extended period. That way I can be a rock, but I am on my way.

Bryan: Well, I hate to break it to you, but whether you are the pastor of a church or not, you are already pastoring people just by your existence and what you have put out there. For those of us who truly know you, you pastor to us all the time. It is not a title, it's your way of life, it's who you are, deep in your core.

Cody: Well, I love you for that and thank you. That is a huge compliment and I receive that for sure. So, I mean, I know it's part of my purpose. We will see how that pans out and where I am supposed to be with that. But it would be a dream for me to be up in the pulpit and being able to bring people to Christ.

Cody is an actor, musician and co-founder/CEO of Circle 11 Entertainment. Instagram: @iamclrose

Justin Paul

Bryan: Were you give a strong foundation in terms of religion/spirituality growing up?

Justin: I absolutely was. My mother was and is the foundation for which all the family's faith and spirituality came from. She was always so close to God, and always tells us how important it was and is, that we pray daily and be steadfast in faith. To this day, whenever my faith is tested, I think about her and steer back toward my relationship with Him. Her convictions have never been as ironclad about anything as they were with faith, and that is something I respect. I see it as my duty, not only to her but myself and Him, to make good on.

Bryan: Was there a time in your teen or young adult life where you felt completely disconnected from God?

Justin: I grew up in a Jewish household. In doing so, I never connected to God from within its structure. I can tell you that the folks who ran the synagogue were so judgmental and always wanting to be seen as so important. In doing so, they came off as arrogant and desiring more for their own egos than they did in imparting knowledge on the young people, or people in general. I was always turned off by their actions and attitudes. As a member of the synagogue and born into the Jewish faith, I'm allowed to say this. After all, I saw them and experienced them with my own eyes all through the time of my youth until I was bar mitzvahed.

I will never forget the way the synagogue treated my family. The way they had my brother pulled from class one day because of a misunderstanding due to what they said was a late payment but really turned out to be a mistake on their part. They had called my mother and had her come pick him up, mid-day, because of what they said was a late payment but was really a processing mistake. My brother and mother were horrified.

Also, the way my mother was pushed out of the choir discretely, which was something she cherished. I will never forget how that community treated my family. That had a lot to do with my displacement in faith, though I can tell you as sure as the nose on my face, I was born to be a Christian.

Here's a secret. As a small boy, I had a very interesting obsession with crosses. I adored them. Drawing them, looking at them…. It was as if I was being called early on, to what is now, and I believe what was always destined to be my Christian backbone. All the while, I was attending Hebrew school and was bar mitzvahed, never having a real sense of faith outside of my mother's teachings and experiences. As it is written, "Many are called, few are chosen". God was always in my heart, but I never truly experienced his love and calling until 2005, when I inexplicably was called by Jesus to become a Christian. To this day, it's the milestone in my life I'm most proud of.

Bryan: What brought you toward Him?

Justin: In short, He did. I was called in a way I can't explain. As a boy I had spent many days sitting in churches; one in particular that was across the street from my house. I felt a sense of calm and peace every time I'd walk in with my skateboard and take a seat. I was always by myself, and just sat quietly. I never told my parents I was there, and I never felt good about being there. One, because I thought I owed it to my parents to be how I was raised, and two, because I felt as though I was intruding in a place I didn't belong. Naturally the conflict that arose from that had me jammed up for years until I was called by Him.

I will never forget going to a church near where I was working at the time, and just sitting there, much like I did when I was a child. Again, I was by myself. I remember saying to myself, "I can't keep coming here like this and not belonging. I need to make this official."

Just like that, I went through the process of Christian Initiation, and for one year I attended classes until Easter of 2006, when I was baptized in the eyes of the Lord. Walter Nolan is the name of the priest who brought me into Christianity. This journey also would not be possible without my godfather, and dear friend, Richard Ryan. Not only was he my right-hand in my sponsorship to Christianity, he was a dear friend and family. He shared his wisdom, wit and even provided me shelter when I needed it. I wouldn't be here today without him.

Bryan: In the entertainment industry, it isn't really "cool" or "hip" to talk about your relationship with God. Have you found a circle of friends who you feel comfortable talking about it with?

Justin: First, anyone in the business who is afraid or in hiding about their faith in what they believe, can never be anyone that leads by example, and is not anyone I would want to associate with. Leaders are real. Leaders come from a place of individuality and pursue their quest despite constant judgment or public opinion. As they say, if you don't have haters, you're doing something wrong. Look at Jesus, who perhaps was the king of that very M.O.

I have still not gotten even remotely close to where I want to be in my acting career. I am not famous, though as I get older, I realize I don't think I want that in my life. I am not rich. I am not able to perform as an actor as a main source of income. I am still working a survival job in the underbelly of Hollywood nightlife while I pursue, now 23 years later, my acting career. I will tell you this: *When* the Lord does bless me with that gift of ascension, when He finally decides to align me with what I believe is my destiny, I will praise His name and let the whole world know. I will do it on any red carpet, any award show, and any opportunity I am blessed with, I will give Him all the glory. He and I have good days and bad. We don't always see eye to eye, as in any relationship, but He is my Lord and Savior, and I will glorify Him to the world when my day does come. Believe that.

Bryan: Do you have Christian brothers that you surround yourself with, in addition to your regular support system of buddies?

Justin: I have a few "conduits" as I call them, who were put in my path to help steer the ship when the seas are rocky. There are three that come to mind specifically. One is a dear friend, Theo, who would come to the hospital with his laptop when I was sick and sit, and play sermons from [Bishop] T.D. Jakes, [Pastor/author] Tony Evans, etc., and never let me let go of God. Any time we'd see one another he'd speak the Word or be there with a DVD for me to watch to receive the message.

The second is a man from the gym who I've come to call "Uncle Mike". He has opened my eyes so much about the ugliness of the modern world, and the Word of The Lord as salvation. He reaches out to me periodically with a daily affirmation, or a word about the Lord, or an excerpt from the Bible. Last time I saw him he invited me to his church that he works for, at a time where I was really going through it. I stood in the back, received the Word, and just cried. He put his hand on my shoulder and told me he'll always be my brother. Another conduit sent by God to keep me on track.

The third one and perhaps the most mystical of all, is a very strange homeless man in Hollywood I befriended named Jericho. He was, by far, the most enigmatic and angelic encounter I have ever had to this day. My first encounter with him was walking to my car one night after work at about 3 a.m. He was panhandling for money around people but didn't ask me for anything as I walked by. *Instead*, he turned, looked at me, and said in what sounded like a Caribbean accent, "Do you believe in love? Because God is love. Brother … God loves *you* so much, don't ever steer away from Him. Nothing is more important than your faith in Him. He will take you where you need to go, you just need to have faith". I was shocked. I couldn't move. He wasn't talking to anyone; just standing there in a recessed doorway of a closed business, and when I walked by, he came to life and looked me dead in my eyes.

I will never forget it, because he seemed out of place; his sweatshirt and jeans were clean, though it was clear through his toes and fingernails he was living in the street and not in a good standing. I gave him $60 that night, thanked him for his words, and kept walking. I thought about that encounter for weeks.

One day weeks later, I was down on my luck and my faith was weak. And that very night, I saw him again. He wouldn't take my money, but he remembered my name, and smiled, thanking me for the money from weeks ago and pointing to the sky. He had asked me if I had been loving God and praying. I told him I was trying but I had fallen so far. He hugged me and whispered in my ear, "You must have faith to please Him. He loves *you* so much. Never lose sight of your relationship with Him. For without Him, there is no love".

Again, my mouth was agape. This happened several times, and always when I was at my lowest; I'd ask him questions and he'd answer with what seemed otherworldly. He would never take my money, so I'd shove 80 or 100 bucks in his pocket when he hugged me and keep on my way. One day he just vanished. Never to be seen again. I believe with all my heart he was sent to deliver a message to me. No one on the boulevard had ever seen him before. When I'd describe him, it was as if he were a ghost.

Bryan: Was there a time in your life that you didn't think you would make it, either in your professional life or personal life, that God pulled you through?

Justin: To be totally honest with you and all who are reading this, that point is right now. I am living it, Bryan. I have never struggled harder than I am right now, but I know it's God's grace that will pull me through and nothing else. I chose a life in the arts that is constantly up and down. You see, to the world, you're just a measly man when you're on your back with nothing to show for your work. No one remembers what you did yesterday, or the day before. It's all about what are you doing now. But mark my words, when I do arrive, everyone will be my "friend" and treat me as if I'm royalty, but the funny thing is I'll still be just a man. I'll just be important for all the wrong reasons to them.

It's all God's will, where we go and how we move on. I have no more right to even be in this book than anyone else. I'd argue there are many that are more deserving, technically, but here we are, God's will.

Bryan: We talked in the first book about your strength, both physically and mentally. How much do you draw on God for that

Justin: All of it. No one has any idea what my day to day is like, both with battling severe sickness/illness that isn't present to the naked eye, as well as rising to the occasion of trying to be more than what the world will just allow me to be. If I told people, they wouldn't believe me. The passion, perseverance, mind-over-matter toughness, and physical overcoming it takes to be great is more than what most are willing to endure. I only can because of His greater plan for my life. I firmly believe that.

Bryan: Do you have a favorite verse or book in the Bible?

Justin: I like the stories about Abraham or David. Basically, any story where man's faith is tested only to be met with God's favor for their faithful display. My favorite book is probably The Book of Job; been feeling a lot like Job lately and it's certainly relative to my life. But we all know how that story ended.

Bryan: Have you been able to help a friend or family member through a challenging time because of your faith in God?

Justin: I can proudly say I was a conduit myself for those that needed me to be on many occasions. It wasn't my doing; it was the Lord calling on *me* to help move someone else the way they needed to be moved. The way God wanted them to be moved. Give and you shall receive, right? I make sure to speak His name as much as I can where it's appropriate. One thing I will say for Hollywood, there is an overwhelming lack of faith. I dare say it's heavily atheist/faithless in more areas than not. Sometimes I can feel that energy on people and I need to get as far from them as possible. Hey, live your life, you know? Just don't bring that my way.

Justin is a native of Princeton, NJ and currently lives in California, where he has worked steadily as an actor. Instagram: @kahnquerall

Gary Casaletto

Bryan: Did you grow up in a religious home?

Gary: I grew up in a very "churched" household. My extended family (Italians are all related, right?) were pastors of a popular Pentecostal church in my hometown. My parents were church leaders, and so all of that had a direct effect on my church life. I am one of those kids that pretty much lived at church every day of the week. Church was both our home and family, and serving the church was our life's purpose. I am grateful because some of my greatest memories and milestones come from my childhood church life.

Bryan: Did you stray from God during your teen/young adult years? If so, what brought you back?

Gary: Yes and no. There are certainly times I have gone through dry seasons where I tried finding fulfillment in the wrong places. However, I never turned away or strayed too far from Him. I think I have needed God so much in my life that I couldn't make it without Him as my anchor.

I have always been "all or nothing" with wherever I channel my life's energy. If God is real, then I believe I am literally created to glorify Him. If Heaven and hell are real, then nothing matters more than relentlessly sharing about this God I know with as many people as I can. I believe with my entire heart that we are each created to glorify God, and each use our unique design to build His kingdom here on Earth.

Bryan: You serve on the youth ministry team at Liquid Church. What made you want to focus on the younger generation?

Gary: Bryan, this is a question I get asked a lot. If I look back at the most impactful times of my life, it would be growing up in kids and youth ministry. Those days are what solidified my core belief system and desire to want to live life with Jesus. It shaped and molded me into a godly man. It helped me spiritually and socially stretch into who I am today. This is where I learned to work with a team and how to grow into a leader. I can honestly say that kids and youth ministry is what developed the confidence and values that have helped me, from being an entrepreneur to leading and serving my family as a father and husband. This experience fuels a passion in me to invest in the younger generations. To hear them, value them and pour into them as they develop into world-changers.

Bryan: Do you have a specific pastoral style?

Gary: Hmmm…. this is a good question. I am a strong apostle in my spiritual gift set. I see a world who needs God and then I see the local church as God's solution to that problem. So put very simply, I have a relentless passion to make the local church the best it can be. I believe that people are called to be the Church. Unfortunately, there is a trend for some churches that put only a few people in leadership and want everyone else to stay in the pews as an audience or to only serve at a low capacity where they are needed and not where their God-given potential is.

I believe the Bible shows that *we are all* called to be the body of Christ and *we all* have been uniquely designed to build His kingdom in some way. I think there are a lot of Christians who attend their local church, but have yet to discover their gifts and passions or have yet to be given the opportunity to grow and use those gifts. Imagine a world where the local church inspired and developed people to empower them to make a difference beyond their own limits. Everything I do from my pastoral style to ministry strategies is about effective discipleship and helping people discover their gifts and make an eternal difference for God.

Bryan: How do you navigate the culture of today as a leader that the younger generation looks to for advice, both spiritual advice and life advice?

Gary: This is a huge question and there are a lot of differing views on this topic. What we can all agree on is that every generation is different from the last. To be a consistent expert in youth ministry is somewhat close to impossible. The truth is our youth can see right through fakeness or inauthenticity. My priority will always be to mirror God and His Word as purely as possible. But that strategy may look different from generation to generation. The vital thing here is that I am not called to prove a point, affirm my pride, or win a popularity contest. I am here to mirror God in a way that brings others closer to Him. I think being real, vulnerable, and honest is a must regardless of the generation. I also believe that this generation specifically needs realness. They want to wrestle with topics and have deep, stretched-out discussions. Not just fall in line with what they are told to do. Creating a space to take the masks off and be vulnerable is a must with our youth.

Bryan: What was an incident in your life that you questioned God's timing or direction you were headed?

Gary: Is this a trick question? I feel like every day I am questioning God's timing. Joking aside, I have countless examples of this in my life and I am sure many others can say the same. There is one that sticks out to me from about three or four years ago. I was serving as a Next Gen Pastor at a thriving church. It was obvious that God was moving, and I was right where He had wanted me. Until I felt God telling me to take a break for a season. It wasn't logical at the time. My ministry was thriving, and I was having some of the most fun I have ever had. But between my business and ministry, I had been going 100 mph for several years. I felt like God was calling me to take a rest and enjoy a season with my wife. This sounds wise, right? Leaders preach about it all the time. But it is not easy. I am a visionary and thrill seeker. I enjoy pioneering new projects and breaking barriers. To leave that was a hit to my pride and identity. I had to learn to find my fulfillment in who God is and not in what I do for Him.

Little did I know what God had in store. Throughout this season I learned more about myself and emotional hurt that had been buried deep inside. My business began to thrive. But most importantly, I prioritized time with my wife and supported her to chase her passions, which was always the other way around. Investing in your spouse is the best return on investment when it comes to living a healthy, fulfilling life.

After a few years, I began to feel a new fire for building the local church ignite inside of me. I put my ear to the ground and entertained some amazing opportunities from outside this state, but felt God calling me to New Jersey. This is when I trusted God with the unknown and joined the staff team with Liquid Family, which turned into my current role as Liquid's Youth and College Pastor. Since being here I have been grateful to not only break some of my greatest fears but somehow also mark off several of my bucket list goals while having the most fun I have ever had. I look back and can see that God was strategically moving in every season I have been in. Sometimes the place He wants to take us is so much bigger than what we can do on our own that the only way to get there is to trust in Him.

Bryan: You have a beautiful family. What are the foundations you and your wife are laying down for your daughter or will you lay down when she is older?

Gary: Thank you so much for that compliment! Every day I admire my wife, Brittany, and daughter Bella and tell myself that I am blessed beyond what I could have ever deserved. Brittany and I often look at each other and just smile in awe that God has blessed us with this child. With that comes the responsibility to lead and parent her well. I believe that discipleship is a parent's role. It's easy to bring our kids to church a few Sundays a year and expect them to be Jesus by the time they graduate high school, but that's definitely not the case. It starts in the home with the family. I believe to lead well as parents we need to be proactive, be relentless about growing and learning, and be intentional about the lifestyle we cultivate.

Right now, these are a few priorities we plan to teach Bella:

1. Relentlessly seek an intimate relationship with God.
2. Relentlessly glorify Him in all she does.
3. Relentlessly love her husband, kids and people God puts in her life.
4. Relentlessly live each season God gives her to the fullest.

These are some values I believe can be found in God's original design for Adam and Eve.

Bryan: What advice would you give to any young person reading this book who feels God/their church is against them for any reason?

Gary: I would say with full confidence that God is not against you. It is the exact opposite. He is not only for you, but values you with a relentless passion beyond what you can even comprehend. I am sorry if the church has poorly mirrored the radically unconditional love of God that we church leaders are just as in need of as you. The Bible shows us that you don't need the approval of the church or of man or even need to change yourself for the love of God. The Bible also shows us that He loves you right here and now regardless of where you are in your journey. If you are reading this, know that you are loved and valued and created on purpose, with a purpose and for a purpose. If you have ever felt hurt by the church or feel God has turned His back on you, then please feel free to contact me on Instagram @garycasaletto, as I would love to give you the opportunity and space to share your story, judgment free!

Gary is the Youth Pastor at Liquid Church and oversees the high school and college students. Gary has over 15 years of experience in church leadership including next gen, urban outreach, communications and church launching. He and his wife, Brittany, are parents to Isabella.

Bryan: Did you grow up with God being at the center of your life?

JP: I was raised in an Episcopalian family that went to church every Sunday. My mom did a great job of getting me to church until I was 14 or 15. Then I became a teenager and rebelled against it. But every Sunday, prior to that, it wasn't even a discussion. We were going, and we were going to be filled with joy while we were there.

Bryan: Was there a reason for the rebellion?

JP: I think that it's natural as a teenager to want to develop your own thoughts and feelings about things. As we commonly see, as a teenager, I rebelled against my parents' authority, and I turned away from Him. I ran wild like a dog off the chain, as they say in the South. I just ran buck wild into whatever trouble I could find.

Bryan: What did that look like for you?

JP: Looking back on it, it was all part of my walk. A lot of times I think about it as like the prodigal son story. I told my parents, "You don't know. I'm smarter than you. I want my inheritance." That to me was my freedom.

Whether it was drinking or just being a very sinful person, everything that I had as a boy, I just turned against that. I was going make my own way. There were days I would go out at night and ended up waking up in pig pens. I had to make my way back.

Bryan: Who was able to bring you back to Him?

JP: My wife, Samantha. We knew each other as children, and I had a heavy-duty crush on her during my childhood. She was my first kiss at five years old. But at age 25, we met back up. When she saw me, she was like, "Oh, my gosh. You're JP. I remember you when we were kids. You chased me around."

One of the first heavy conversations she had with me was telling me that God had a bigger plan for me and that I should turn to Him for guidance. In my head I am thinking, "What does that even mean?" She told me that I should own up to my failures, stupid choices and ask Him for His help.

She took me to a Jennifer Knapp concert. I thought it was going to be at a bar, but it was during the Dove Awards, which unbeknownst to me, was a Christian music awards show. She was a dancer in the Christian music industry. We went and I heard this music that felt like it had been written right onto my heart.

Jennifer was sitting on a stool with a light coming down from above. It was top lit, like a dramatic police interrogation, and it was just her with an acoustic guitar. I just wept. Tears ran down my face as if I had no control. I said to my Samantha, "What is going on?" She looked at me and said "Oh, that's the Holy Spirit. It's time. Your heart is saying words that your brain is not listening to, and they are having a battle. God is in it, and He wants you."

Suddenly, I realized that God had been with me in every single pig pen, every single mess I'd made, every decision that had gone in the wrong direction and that He had never left me. But instead, He was there with me holding up my head out of the pig pen. He was not pointing his finger at me. That, instead, He had his hands wide open, opening His arms to me like a father gives a hug.

Bryan: That is definitely something you and I have in common. Worship music always hits me. After losing my brother, I remember Clint Taylor singing, "Same God" at our staff meeting and I completely lost it, but also connected in a different way than it had prior. There are many worship songs that have brought me to tears or have gotten me hyped up.

JP: I had a Youth Pastor at my church, St. Bartholomew's in Nashville, Tennessee, named Tom Rutherford, who made a great impact on me. He wore flip-flops, had a beard and was cool and he played music.

I made the decision to move to California to start over and get away from my old life and partying. As soon as I got there, I got a job at a record label, and it was amazing. In my wildest dreams, I never knew that I was wired for that. My thought process is when someone gives you something, you say, "Thank you". But how do I thank God for something so huge? I didn't even know about tithing at the time, so I decided I can give him my time. Maybe there are a lot of little JPs out there that I can talk to and help. Or maybe there are some Samanthas along the way that we can catch before they fall off the rails.

I made a plan with my wife, wherever we are and whatever season we're in and whatever age we are, to mentor those below us. Whether it's middle schoolers, teenagers, or young couples about to get married. We want to give thanks to God with our service. That helps us remember to be thankful. Hopefully, along the way, all those little JPs and Samanthas don't get left behind.

Bryan: Were there any times working in the music industry where your job did not align with your beliefs?

JP: There have been countless situations where things were going on that did not align with my art and my Lord. The way I approach all that is, early on in my relationships with artists, record labels and managers, I just let them know that I am a youth pastor, youth mentor and I am married. I don't do any drugs. I don't drink. But I'm going to work hard for you, and you can trust me. If you need me to do all those things that people assume you have to do in the music business to be successful, then you're talking to the wrong person.

But if you want someone to work with you, to understand your heart, and to push you to be the best version of yourselves you can be, whether that is as an artist or a husband, man, or a woman, then I am your right person. I won't lie to you and won't sell down. If you are wild, out partying and it is affecting what we need to create, I will let you know.

There have been times where people have tried to get me to be in situations where I shouldn't be. There have been awkward times when very famous people have had to say, "He doesn't roll like that. He goes home. He doesn't go to the club with us," or whatever it is. If I start off with letting people know what's in my heart and in my mind and who my Lord is, then they respect that most of the time.

Now it's not to say that there have not been some problems along the way. Some people can't deal with that. When they have their own guilt and their own issues with sin, sometimes they're not comfortable with me. I have had people bring young girls in their 20s to me as interns and I just have to say, "No, thank you". I don't want an intern that is going be around me that is a young woman and is attractive. I would prefer that woman be mentored by another woman.

I have that from some of the great pastors that I have had in my life. They never give Satan a doorway. That is tough and sometimes people don't understand it. I feel like if you were to ask people about me, that they would say, "He's a Christian. Yeah, he's a married man, 22 years. He's a great father. He's a mentor. He helps others, and that dude won't do these things. But he does a great job anyways." That is what you want in life. By pushing aside that may cause me to stumble or cause other people to stumble, I've been able to protect my marriage, my sobriety, and my relationship with God.

Bryan: How do you approach the many difficult issues that surround young people today when you are mentoring them?

JP: Right now, we've got a lot of questions about identity and who I am and where I should be and what I should do and so forth. My number one job is to create a path for others to find God. So, when I have a student come to me with questions about identity and where they fit into the culture, I point them to God.

I let them know that where you are when you're 15 is not where you are when you're 20 or 25 or 30 or 40. Having questions of identity or where you fit into culture or sin or drugs or whatever, that's normal. Everybody's got questions.

But if you have a line of communication with God, He will steer you in the right direction always. Sometimes that fogginess that's in the mirror when we're trying to talk to God is not God covering up who He is, but really, culture fogging up what we need to see. I have parents who come to me, and I tell them the number one job that you can do is create a personal relationship with Jesus. That's the number one job. That will cement them in their life more than anything you can say or do.

Bryan: I can imagine that goes over much better than flat out telling them they are wrong and telling them what to do.

JP: Yes, or being ignorant. I don't have the perfect answer to all the world's problems. I know that God says lots of different things in the Bible to us. If we don't have the relationship with God to even feel comfortable picking up the Bible, no matter what version it is, then we can't really listen to them.

I often tell people that God does not want you to judge others, He wants you to bring them to Him. You can't have that same open hug with your hands wide open if your finger is pointing or in a fist.

I attended a conference that Andy Stanley was speaking at, and he said something to the effect that our job is to give kids, young adults, and adults the safest place that they can come and share with you, their questions. If they can't even share what's on their mind because you've judged them in so many different ways, then you've failed them.

Look at how we have treated divorce in the past. There are certain places where you're not comfortable if you've been divorced. Parents aren't perfect, just like young adults. If people are in a marriage that's unsafe or sinful or whatever, you can't hold divorce against them. Instead, you've got to fortify them. If you're so busy throwing stones at people, you can't put the stones around the foundation of their life.

One time in the music business, somebody was talking about a band. And they said, "Oh, hell hath no fury like a Christian who feels scorned. And that band, blah, blah, blah, blah, blah." This was in a big conference room with a giant table and tons of people. Then they whipped around, and they were like, "No offense, JP, because I know you're one of them." It is one of the biggest record labels in the world, and their HR department called me within 15 minutes. They said, "Oh, we just want to make sure that you feel supported. We know that you were mocked for your faith and that's not okay. We want you to fill out paperwork and we are going to go after this person, and we are going to have them fired on your behalf."

Now, this person may or may not be a great person. It's not my job to judge them. But I said to that HR person, and I've lived with it my whole life, and I answered him biblically and said, "Listen, let the person that goes without sin throw that first stone. It's not going be me."

Bryan: Did that surprise them?

JP: They were like, "Excuse me, what?" They had never heard anything like that in their life in an HR conversation. I probably could have gotten tons of money and a settlement or whatever they wanted to do. But I said no because every single person that that person ever encountered, everyone in that room, maybe even that band, everyone, from then on, would say, "Oh, he was right. Those Christians are horrible."

But instead, I reflected God's love, forgiveness, and grace back. I think that that was a bolder, wiser, bigger conversation for them.

Bryan: I love that because Christians do tend to get lumped together with the loudest voices screaming things in the name of Christianity.

JP: Oh, yeah. People have their guard up all around us. They're ready to fight. We have to remember that someone before us, maybe when they were a kid or maybe at school or anywhere along the way, someone said you're not right, you're broken, you're wrong, you're all these things. As a Christian, when we show grace, it really transcends their anger.

Bryan: You also have a passion for working with the homeless and with City Relief.

JP: They are some of our best forgotten citizens. I really feel like they had been dealt a bad hand. I felt like society does not want to look at them or see them and doesn't want to deal with the homeless. There are a lot of great people at City Relief who have their hands wide open in a hug, and it was just amazing to me.

When Covid hit and everything was closing, our homeless were being affected more by Covid than ever because they relied on other people for services. They didn't really have the same choices that we had. They couldn't quarantine like we could. They did not have the savings or family to fall back on. They were kind of alone in this. That just made me emotionally connected with them. I wanted them to know that I didn't feel they were any different than anyone else. I wanted to show them the same grace, the same love, and the same support that God had given me no matter what I was saying or doing in my youth. I just went out and I made artwork for them that said, "You are loved. You're perfect the way you are. You are beautiful. You are seen."

They may have had interactions with their family or other Christians that were not positive and may have their guard up. My "job" is to have the conversation that Jesus would have if he bumped into him. It is important to address them by their name because they do not have an identity on the street. On the street, they may have a nickname or no name at all. A lot of people don't make eye contact. So, I found myself having to take my sunglasses off so they can see my eyes.

I would be so excited to go into the city every Wednesday and I would set up and paint all day making art. Then, we would put it out on social media and some of the art would sell. We would give that money directly to City Relief. I think I went for 30 weeks, whether it was raining or cold. I have painted in snowshoes one time in three feet of snow. It was amazing and it was just a great experience. It really reoriented my compass.

Even my kids and people in the community would get involved. I just could not believe how awesome people were and how open they were to helping others, when you give them the chance. Not everyone can go into the city and give up a day, but it is amazing to do. I would even tell my clients that I was unreachable on Wednesdays.

Bryan: How important is it to have Christian brothers on your walk with God?

JP: It is super-important. That is one of the ways Liquid has been great with me. Iron sharpens iron and you can be in any season you want, and you may not feel like you could sharpen anyone's iron. When you open your eyes and your heart, there's always people you can help. It has been great to have strong married men around me that are on a similar walk and holding each other accountable.

It is great to know that whether you are in a season where your storehouse is super-full or in a drought, you're able to help or receive help from other people. I am thankful for the men's groups and the men's workdays or even going paintballing or snowboarding.

You have got to get around people that can hold you accountable because if you're one way six days out of the week and then a different way on Sunday, eventually those other days are going creep up on you.

One of the pastors came up to me and asked if I wanted to lead a men's group. I asked them, "Why me?" They said because I have had to walk through fire, so it would be great if I would lead.

I was able to pause life a little bit and get down to helping others. I look back on those times as another way that God has blessed me. Another word that He has imprinted on my heart. I guess that would be a "mentor".

Bryan: Is it easier for your children to come to you seeing you mentor other young adults?

JP: I think that we're always going to have teenagers wanting to create their own life, their own beliefs and their circles of friends and influence. It is easier for me to speak into someone else's kids when the conversation is difficult than it is for me to speak into my own children on a difficult topic. I will speak into it, but whether they listen to it or not is a different story.

What Sam and I have found is, the same iron sharpen iron in terms of men, iron sharpens iron applies to families. Some of those families can help with your kids as well. I've had lots of kids that I mentor or families that we share our faith with speak into our kids and tell them things that I have said a thousand times.

Bryan: Why do you think it is easier to have conversations with other people's kids?

JP: I think that at a certain age, our kids think that we don't know everything. I think that other people's influence is seen as a little bit wiser. Sometimes kids just rebel against authority or what they believe to be true.

My kids in no way are rebellious or awful, but they call me Youth Pastor Kevin sometimes when I sound too strong. They're like, "All right, Youth Pastor Kevin. So, what do you say we just dial down the ministry and turn up the fun dad?" And I'm like, "Well, sometimes I have had hard conversations with you."

JP is the creative director at Composite.is (www.composite.is). He volunteers for City Relief and is very active in the youth ministry at Liquid Church. He and his wife, Samantha, are parents to daughter Stevie and son Jackson.

Josh Santibanez

Bryan: You are very convicted in your faith. What led you to that?

Josh: Who I am as a person, my world views, ideologies, and even my Christian faith is because of my father. I am who I am because of him and not just through my genetics and personality, as well as my conviction.

I know that now, but when I was younger it was like, "Why is my dad a pastor? Why is my dad a Christian? Why does he have these diehard beliefs that if someone pointed a gun to his head, he would still confess that there's only one true God?"

I never understood that until I was older. That was when I started questioning things, like my dad is preaching God is good, but my mom got breast cancer. I have a younger brother, Benjamin, who has Angelman syndrome, which is a genetic neurological disorder and anything that controls muscle movement doesn't work.

My dad would be happy, joyful, hugging people and preaching about how good God is, but I saw it differently. I came to the realization that my dad was not overlooking what is happening, but it is that he knows these things have a purpose, and that suffering is part of life. What my dad modeled so well was that despite life having bad situations, there is a good God that really loves us, is in control and if we let Him take over, we find purpose.

When my mother had breast cancer, that served a purpose for me. She was healed after doctors gave her six months to live. Even for my little brother, they said that he would never speak or do anything at all, but I would see my father pray for him and then months later, he would say "Mom," which is not supposed to be possible. That led me to having more faith in God, believing in a higher power and divine intervention.

I was about to turn 18 and I was standing in my bedroom and literally said to God, "If you're real, show me something. Give me a sign." My heart was beating so fast waiting for something to happen. I am not sure what I thought would be that sign. Would it be cinematic, like a big thunderstorm directly over the house, God speaking to me in a Morgan Freeman voice, or something dramatic? None of that happened, but I was still expectant. I didn't fall asleep that night. By 3 a.m. I was mad at God. I was like, "Dude, you say you're real. My dad says you're real. You don't demonstrate yourself. I'm pissed."

I was so angry, the only thing I could do is exercise to get tired and fall asleep. I went for a run and asked God for a sign. I started seeing the sun rise and a voice in me was like, "Do you see all of this creation? Do you see how I set the sunrise? I make it do that. I created all these things." I heard the birds chirping and saw nature.

Then what really blew my mind and made me a Christian was not all that evidence of God [but] the only thing that He can't control is me. He can control the storms, He can control nature, He can control cosmic things to happen, but He created me with a free will, and He created someone that might not want Him.

At that time, I didn't know what I was feeling, but now I know that it was the Holy Spirit. I got chills all over my body. I started crying non-stop. By this point people were jogging in the park as well and a woman stopped and asked if I was okay. Ever since that day, my life changed.

Bryan: That all happened near the end of your teenage years. Prior to that, were you getting into trouble, or rebelling because you were a pastor's kid?

Josh: I don't know how many pastor's kids you've interviewed, Bryan, but there are statistics that state that one of the main reasons kids of pastors leave the faith is because of that fact. I think there are other reasons, like a pastor preaches Christian values at church, but then at home he is a terrible husband and/or father. That was not my experience. My father acted the same regardless of whether he was in the church, in our home or out in society.

When I was in middle school, I saw a lot of kids that were more well-versed in the Bible than I was. Instead of learning the teachings and the background, I turned to memorization. I believed if I did that, when I was in church people would not see the real me and would just see me as a nice young son of the pastor.

But in school, I was a totally different kid. I started bullying, started being mean and I started cussing. I started grabbing toilet paper, mushing it up with water, throwing it onto the ceiling and throwing it at the teacher. During church services, I would slash the deacon's car tires.

I felt so much pressure being a pastor's kid to live up to that title. I fell into a season of hating the church. I saw the hypocrisy. I saw people talking about my father. Even my own friends would say that my father was stealing or that he had special benefits just because he was pastor.

That started making me feel isolated and I started to not talk to my father. I would just be in my room and even Psych 101 would tell you the first sign of depression is isolation. In those moments of isolation, I fell into pornography and was addicted to porn when I was 13 or 14 years old. I got indulged in pornography so hard that literally till this day, I am suffering the consequences of the images that I saw, the things I was tempted to do, the way I viewed women or even the way I would approach a girl. I wouldn't approach girl because she was pretty. It was because I wanted to take advantage of her. The entire persona of being a "good pastor's son" went down the drain when I let that be the definition of who I was. It was really scary.

I did a lot of damage when I was in high school. To this day, friends of friends can't believe that I'm a youth pastor or that I am in a ministry position. They are like, "There's no way. Josh did this to me, or tried to do this with me, or treated me in a certain way." I'm only 26 years old now, so it really has not been that long since it happened or for people to forget.

Bryan: When you had your come-to-God moment, what did you do to change, and what led you to wanting to be a pastor?

Josh: When I turned 18 years old, I was about to graduate high school, and I felt God persuaded me to come clean to my father about my pornography addiction. I was scared to tell him because he has always been this great figure to model myself after and I felt like I let him down. When I told him, he said that he was not angry at me and was happy that I told him so we could work it out together.

He guided me out of that dangerous season. He would block the porn websites and got wi-fi security. Even then I would look around to see if the password was written down somewhere on a piece of paper. My dad ultimately cut my internet services because of that. If I was letting my father down that much, it could have only been worse in God's eyes.

I ultimately did a prayer of repentance and dove into His word. From that point on my relationship with my father only got better when I accepted Jesus Christ as Lord and my Savior.

I fell in love with the Bible, and every time I would read it, for some reason it would make me a different person. I started praying more and talking to people about Jesus. I was 19 years old when I got assigned to be a youth pastor at my father's church.

My father threw me in the fire, basically. I did everything I could to be the best I could be at what God was calling me to be in that position. I went to seminars, took courses, went to conferences, and did Bible studies with my father for hours at a time. I did almost two years of seminary with Assembly of God. I fell in love with this next generation, and I loved how kids were coming to me.

Bryan: You mentioned how others reacted when they heard you had chosen God over the secular, but how did your friends react to you becoming a Youth Pastor?

Josh: They did not believe me. They said I was just doing it to cover up all the bad that I had done and since I could not fix the past, I was trying to cover it. That was hurtful to me because those were people that cared about me.

But what they didn't realize was that God literally transformed me. The Bible says that when we accept Jesus in our hearts, we become a new creation. Sometimes, it's so new that you don't even recognize yourself or others don't even recognize you because of how new you have become.

I started falling in love with ministry. I met my beautiful wife when I was on the verge of turning 20 and we got married super early. I have been to several preaching engagements. I've worked with other pastors in the region. Now I am in the process of trying to launch my own church.

Bryan: What would that look like for you?

Josh: I would try to be as different as possible. Obviously, I would not be compromising any convictions or Biblical truths, but it would be very, very nontraditional. I believe that church is a hospital. It's not a place for people that don't need help. A church is a place of imperfect people, and scripture says that we are the temple, that we are the church. That is something that I believe this generation needs. They do not need perfect people. They need people with a broken past which is relatable. If they can see examples of what God can do, then maybe they can start believing it for themselves.

I just need to make sure that the love that Jesus expressed and was so relatable, that I need to have that. What made Jesus relatable is that He was human. He had a dialogue. He had an attitude of a servant. One of the last things that He did before He died on the cross was that He washed the disciples' feet. We're talking about a divine being, a perfect person kneeling as if He were imperfect. My job is to love people as much as I can and to share truth as much as I can. It's God's job to save them. I need to be a messenger. You can be a bigger influence over someone's life more when you have integrity and authority over the things that you believe.

Bryan: Your generation deals with so much, whether it is sex, drugs, alcohol, gender, sexuality distinctions, etc. How do you come from a heart posture and not seem like an insensitive person when facing the challenges that are coming at young people today?

Josh: That is the best question of all time because this isn't just a culture problem. Throughout Genesis, it talks about knowing how to manage what God says and be obedient to those teachings. But in that is where I feel that is why more than ever, we need to follow what Jesus did. There is no secret way of doing that. There is just learning and becoming like someone that did that already, and his name is Jesus.

My job on this Earth is to be as much like Jesus as possible. Jesus is the perfect model. The way Jesus talked to people and addressed sin was so lovingly and compassionately. Look at John 8:7 where Jesus tells all the people ready to stone the adulterous woman, "He that is without sin among you, let him cast the first stone at her. After Jesus said that everyone dropped their stones.

But what I love about Jesus is that He protected before He corrected. Instead of bashing the woman in public, Jesus protected her. He then instructs her to live without sin. Right off the bat, we see two tensions. On one hand, she is a human being, and she's in the image of God. We need to protect people like that.

But at the same time, Jesus is the truth, the way, and the life. He had to share truth. Jesus is always going to be on the side of caring for you. But He cares so much for you that He will never leave you despite your sin.

Bryan: How do you navigate through people's reactions to what you say?

Josh: I care more about God than what people think of me. That is not being mean. That's just being thoughtful and being in a position where the moment I stop caring what God thinks, I will bow down to culture and to what society thinks. I am way more concerned about the person knowing who they're called to be in Jesus, rather than me finding affirmation in anything else.

I have heard it put this way: We like what God doesn't like, and God likes what we don't like. Unfortunately, because of sin, it's in our nature to do things that we want to do. Anything that gets in the way of what I want is seen as an enemy, and that's the culture of today.

If you don't identify me as what I want you to, if you don't treat me the way I want you to, if you don't talk to me the way I want you to, then you don't love me. Or if you don't agree with me or the things I want you to agree with me, then you don't love me. What I love about Jesus is that He expressed convictions and He spoke about sin so much that He would demonstrate and care for you at the same time.

Bryan: There has been a lot of church hurt in the past.

Josh: I'm always the first one saying, "Look, I'm so sorry what the church did." There are terrible, terrible things that the church has done under God's name, but there's also another spectrum of so many good things that came out of the church. Out of the church came the concept of abolishing slavery, about equality, about social justice, all those moral and ethical values that we hold today.

Whether you're an atheist or not, the whole Constitution of the United States was signed by people that had faith in God. They had a world view of what the Bible said because back then Bibles were in schools. Back then, you were allowed to pray. Even our dollar bills say, "In God we trust."

My calling for this next generation is to not be the savior of what the church did in the past but to be the best example of who we can be in the way Jesus was. That's it.

Bryan: My baptism was the first time I feel like I had a supernatural experience in Him. I have had a few more since. Have you?

Josh: I have had two. The first one was when I got baptized and then got baptized in the Spirit because the Bible does differentiate both. Being baptized in the Holy Spirit, for everyone each experience is different. For me it was a constant awareness that God is always with me.

The second one was having prophetic insight. Prophetic insight is not about knowing things about the future but knowing of things that I shouldn't know about that God shares with me. He trusts me to present that in a way of not that "God hates you" but from a place of "God sees you".

I went to the mall one time, and we were in the Pandora store because my wife was looking to add a charm to her collection. One of the saleswomen asked if she could help, and I told her we were just looking. She said to just let her know if at any point that she could. At this point I got a weird thought in my head about the name Alexis or Alexandra. It took me by surprise. Since I am an extrovert and love talking to people, I don't have a problem saying "weird" or "out there" things to people. The same saleswoman comes up and she starts telling us about the deals that they have. My heart started beating really fast and I wondered if I should say something to her. I decided to ask her if the name Alexis or Alexandra meant anything to her.

Her eyes opened wide and a tear came down. At that moment I got more information and asked if the Alexis or Alexandra was her sister. At that point she started freaking out and asking who I was. I told her not to get weirded out, that I was a Christian and I believe in God. I also believe that God talks to people and shares intimate detailed information with others, just to let people know He loves them and sees them. She said, "That is impossible. She lives in Spain, and there's no way you would know that about her." And I go, "Yeah, but God knows." Then I told her I felt like God gave me her name because she missed her, that she was feeling neglected and depressed because your sister was your best friend. And she just starts crying.

I said to her, "Look, I don't know anything about you. We're complete strangers. But I do know something. God loves you so much that a perfect stranger came into your store, tells you this intimate detail just to say, "I love you and I see you." At that moment she says, "Okay, what just happened changed everything I believe about God."

Bryan: You and Sarah have been married for six years. Was starting a family part of your hope for the future?

Josh: Yes. When we were dating, she told me that she couldn't have kids. I really didn't mind. I just thought we would always adopt, which by the way is still something I still want to do. But we started trying anyway.

Sarah did end up getting pregnant, but three or four months in we had a miscarriage. That was also another dark season of my life where I started reevaluating what I believed in and what my convictions were at that time. That is what the enemy loves to do. The enemy tries to test your convictions and tries to grab earthly facts. I started believing that lie for a season of my life, and that's where I realized my feelings and these earthly facts can't wipe away everything that God has done in my life and the convictions that I believe. Because if that is the case, if God's truth can be easily wiped away based on earthly facts, then He isn't God, He isn't who He says He is. Because He's the absolute truth despite whatever feelings or whatever things we might have. We went to our last resort, which was the IVF process. That was a full year of torture honestly. The injections, the hormonal changes, the pain that my wife felt. Her psychological traits even started changing because you're injecting yourself with hormones. It was very rough in the beginning, and we started to think it was not worth it. But we stuck it out. The doctor told us that it could take about four or five tries of IVF treatments to get pregnant. By the grace of God, she is now pregnant with our son, who is due in December of 2022. We are very grateful to Him.

Josh is part of the pastoral team at HOW Church (House of Worship Church - https://howchurch.org/ and co-hosts The Safe podcast - safepodcast.buzzsprout.com. Josh and his wife, Sara, are expecting a son this December. Instagram: @josh_santibanez

Bryan: You were raised in a spiritually strong household, correct? What do you recall being the foundation your parents laid out for you?

Alex: Yes, I grew up in a Christian household going to church every Sunday, and both my parents were heavily involved in ministry. They both helped start the previous church that we went to. Church was like a second home because we spent so much time there. At home, my parents were always playing worship music around the house. They made time to read the Bible to me and my siblings and had us watch *VeggieTales.* These core moments helped form the basis of my faith today. My parents stressed how important going to church was, and when I was five years old, I accepted Jesus as my savior, although it wasn't until I was much older that I feel like I really made my faith my own.

Bryan: Was there a time in your early mid-teens where you went through a rebellious stage in terms of your spirituality/walk with Him?

Alex: Yes. When I was in middle school and high school, I wanted very little to do with church. I saw religion as just a bunch of rules and it seemed like all my friends were having a better time than me. I found church boring and honestly thought I was wasting my time. I saw God and His rules to be limiting my freedom in what I could do, instead of guidelines protecting me from unhealthy consequences.

In high school especially, what I cared about most was fitting in and trying to be the most popular kid in school. A lot of my friends were making unwise decisions and walking down a path counter to the Christian faith. It was easier to go along with them than it was to set myself apart and focus on my walk with the Lord.

Despite all that, I tried to stay out of trouble and always had a voice inside telling me right from wrong. Years later, I realized that it was the Holy Spirit guiding me and trying to keep me from going down the wrong path. I am grateful that God never gave up on me and kept pursuing me even when I wanted nothing to do with Him.

Bryan: How have you navigated the challenges of being a young adult today with all the difficult issues being put in front of today's young people?

Alex: First and foremost, it is incredibly important to spend time praying and having alone time with God. Having a time of silence and solitude at the beginning of my day is crucial to better hear from God and root myself in His presence to start the day. Instead of checking my phone or going on social media, I try to spend this quality time with God to further our relationship and in turn, He fills me with his comfort and peace.

I don't have any social media at all, and a big part of why is because I didn't want something competing for my attention with God. Additionally, I take the time to open His word and remind myself of the truths that *He* says about me versus what the world will tell me. This helps me combat any anxiety, worry, or lies that the enemy tries to convince me about myself.

Another important thing to help navigate the challenges of being a young adult is being a part of a small group. It's so important to be a part of a healthy community and having people my age around me who are also believers to encourage and support me through the mountains and valleys of life.

No matter what stage of life you are in, you need community to thrive, but especially as a young person in today's world. My college small group at Liquid gave me a place to share my faith with like-minded people, to be held accountable and to just have fun. This allowed me to grow, ask questions and wrestle with my faith in the comfort and safety of knowing I have brothers and sisters going through the same issues.

Bryan: Have you ever had an issue with a friend that led to disagreements with your views versus theirs? How did you resolve the issue?

Alex: Yeah, I remember in high school I got into an argument with a teammate because he was making fun of a kid on our soccer team. It started off as just a few comments, but then it eventually grew to an everyday thing and some of the team started stealing/messing with his belongings and things. I spoke up and told them to stop, and thankfully, they did.

However, one of my teammates didn't see what the big deal was, and even asked me, "Why would you take his side, he's such a loser!" Hearing that broke my heart even more, and it showed me we had very different ways of looking at people.

Because of the radical love I received from Jesus, love I don't deserve, I try to share kindness and love to every person I meet. I'm not perfect, nor do I claim to be, but I could tell this teammate didn't understand where I was coming from. However, that didn't mean I should give up there.

After that encounter, I tried to spend intentional time with my teammate who was getting bullied, whether it was hanging out, inviting him to sit with us at lunch, or just asking him how his day was going. I hoped that this made him feel seen and loved, but also showed my teammates that didn't like him that it was worth getting to know him and spend time with him. Eventually, I feel like my teammates came around and were much more kind to this kid, and I hope what I did, even if it was small, helped.

Bryan: At Liquid Church, you are heavily involved in the young adult's ministry. How did that ministry help you throughout high school and college?

Alex: At the beginning of high school, I joined a life group for the first time, not knowing what to expect, but it ended up being one of the best decisions I've ever made. It gave me the opportunity to meet so many new people (many of whom became some of my best friends and still are today) and allowed me the space to talk about my faith journey and wrestle with challenges that come with being a young follower of Christ.

When I started college, I decided it was important to find the same type of community, and so I joined the first college small group at Liquid! This group has grown my faith in ways I could never imagine. After a year of attending, I was asked to take over and lead the group, which has further deepened my faith in Jesus and taught me what it means to truly care for those around me. I've had to lean on Him even more every day in order to be a good leader. Being rooted in these communities throughout my fundamental years shaped me into the person I am today.

Bryan: Who has been a mentor on your walk with God? What did they instill in you?

Alex: I have been very blessed to have several mentors throughout my life, but my youth pastor Jonathan Wilson has been a key factor in my walk with Jesus. He has encouraged me in so many different ways and has enabled me to start seeing myself the way God sees me. He has given me so many opportunities to lead and step out of my comfort zone so that I can also make a difference for the next generation. He has been a great role model for me to follow and is someone of the highest integrity and character. He has taught me so much, and I'm forever grateful for that. He has shown me what a true man of God looks like and what it means to live a life for others. That's something I want to aspire to do.

Bryan: How have you been able to use your love for God and others?

Alex: I have the privilege of serving every week on our Liquid Family team. I volunteer in the elementary classroom, caring for the next generation by teaching them about Jesus in an environment filled with fun and games. I have been able to form a special bond with those kids and watch them start to develop a faith of their own. I also serve at Parents Night Out with our special needs ministry, which are nights that celebrate kids with special needs and their families.

Nothing brings me more joy every week than seeing their faces and knowing that I'm making a difference in their lives. In return, I am filled with the amazing feeling that comes with putting someone else before myself.

Bryan: Do you have any interest in becoming a youth pastor/pastor?

Alex: I think it could be a possibility in the future if the opportunity presented itself at the right time. I'm grateful for all the mentors, youth pastors, and pastors that have poured into me and helped mold my faith in Christ, and I would love the chance to do the same for someone else.

Bryan: What does it mean to be a good Christian?

Alex: I would say being a good Christian simply means putting God first in everything you do. The words we speak and the actions we take should reflect the same behavior Jesus Christ modeled for us. One of the passages of scripture I come back to most is Galatians 5, verses 22-25, which talks about the fruits of the spirit and how to live. "But the fruit of the Spirit is love, joy, peace, forbearance, kindness, goodness, faithfulness, gentleness, and self-control. Against such things there is no law. Those who belong to Christ Jesus have crucified the flesh with its passions and desires. Since we live by the Spirit, let us keep in step with the Spirit."

Keeping in step with the spirit should be the ultimate goal for us as "good" Christians. We will never be able to measure up to the example Jesus set and we will always fall short, but lucky for us, God's grace covers us because of the sacrifice Jesus gave at the cross. But now it's our job to do our best to live in a way that glorifies Him and leaves non-believers wondering what makes us different. Scripture says we are called to be the light of the world, so let's be that to everyone we meet!

Bryan: Finally, what advice would you give to someone around your age who is struggling with their faith in today's culture?

Alex: I would say never give up on your faith and never give up on God even when life seems too difficult. Even in trying times, God is always right by your side, wanting the best for you and arranging things behind the scenes for your good. Trying times don't mean you're far from God; in fact, they are the situations where God's power can shine through brightest.

One of my favorite sayings is, "Sometimes God lets you hit rock bottom so you will discover that *He* is the *Rock* at the bottom." He is our strength in difficult times. Don't be afraid to stand out or to stick up for what is right. Do your best to make God the number one priority in your life and aim to glorify Him in everything you do. Our world will try to put you down or tell you that you're not worth it, but it is important to remember that God loves you and has a unique purpose for your life. This will lead to a fulfilling life beyond what you could have ever hoped for or imagined.

Alex currently serves as the Campus Manager at Liquid Church's Morris County location and works with the young adult ministry.

Nate & Amanda Goyco

Bryan: Did you grow up in a home where church attendance and God were central to family life?

Nate: Absolutely. I grew up in a church where almost everyone was family. My dad was the worship pastor, and I grew up in ministry since I was a kid. God was always the center of everything we did as a family together.

Amanda: Not really. I grew up Catholic. We believed in God and knew He was important, but church attendance was not the main priority growing up, unless you count Easter and Sunday school classes.

Bryan: It's not uncommon for kids and teens to not be "into" church. Was that how both of you were?

Nate: I was sadly one of those kids. I knew about God, and I called myself a Christian, but I was not serious about church. I would slack off like kids usually do and get into a deep hole. But He was always there.

Amanda: I did not think church was cool growing up. It was more embarrassing, especially when my grandma put me in Sunday school. I never understood why it was important to her because we never went to church much.

Bryan: When did God place it on your heart to take it more seriously?

Nate: I started to take it seriously at the age of 13. I was at a conference called Battle Cry in New Jersey. A pastor named John Gray was doing a sermon. During his sermon, he started worshipping and singing. Right then and there, I heard God speak to me, "I am here". I fell to my knees, lifted my hands, and started crying. Right at that moment is when I experienced my first encounter and started taking it seriously.

Amanda: When I was about 15 years old and started going to a Christian church. It was a different atmosphere for me. I was going through a dark time, and I was tired of feeling alone. So, I gave my heart to the Lord and knew this was going to be a lifetime of pursuing Him.

Bryan: How did you guys get together and was each of you being strong Christians important to the other? Was that always the case even prior to meeting?

Nate: Neither of us were considered strong Christians. I was still going through my ways, as was she, but we kept God in our relationship. We attended church together, but sat separately before we were dating, but we loved to worship all the time. Prior to meeting, for me it was that they had to know God, but I never took it that seriously. It was whoever I had an emotional connection to, and I loved from the inside. I got lucky because once we started dating, God took over both of our lives.

Amanda: We met at youth ministry and as all teens do, Nate slid into my DMs. I knew being a Christian and following God was important to him. But in that stage of my life, I wasn't there yet. We remained friends for two years as I continued my walk and growth in God. He encouraged me in that season. When the time was right for us both, we decided to see how it would be as a couple, putting God in the center of our relationship. It was confirmed we needed to be together, and we never looked back.

Bryan: What I love about both of you is even though you are still young, you both are very strong in your faith, which many people your age are still questioning or figuring it out. What challenges has that brought to you in relationships with your peers?

Nate: One of the many challenges that we face is peers telling us we are too young. People always assume that because we are young, we are not fully mature, that we don't have it together or our marriage will never last. That is absolutely false. If you love the person for who they are and have a deep love for each other that is everlasting, God placed the both of you together to be forever. Nothing will happen to the relationship if God is in the center.

Amanda: The pressure is on! People don't understand that yes, we're young, but we are in a completely different mindset than a regular person in their 20s. But because we are in a different part of life, we can give them advice in something that we may have already experienced because we grew up quicker than normal. Show them that God is literally the key to everything. We are a living testimony that He comes through for His children. For someone my age who's probably in school, living at home, still dating, certain times may feel like the end of the world. But I am here to remind them of what He can do and what He has done in our lives. I will give Him glory and share my testimony any day.

Bryan: How did God help you through challenges that arose as you were dating and subsequently married?

Nate: We prayed, we started doing devotionals, but we always said to each other, God is in this, and we would never be where we are without Him.

Amanda: God definitely taught me how to love when you're in darkness. I was dealing with the loss of my grandmother when we started dating. At that time, I wanted to hide in a hole, but God showed me the true meaning of love is patient, kind, and is slow to anger through Nate. Prayer and being completely transparent got us through the worst season of my life, especially being such a young couple.

Bryan: As our friendship has deepened, I have obviously seen the love between you, but I am sure every day is not rainbows and puppies. How do you guys work through issues?

Nate: We have ups and downs just like every marriage does. We do have some really bad days, but we always communicate. The main thing is communication. It took years for us to fully develop our communication skills with each other and talk about things correctly. I was more of the, "I don't want to talk about it" type. She was the talker and wanted to talk about it, and that conflicted heavily between us because things were swept under the rug a lot. We started talking more, started communicating more, and started talking like regular married people about our issues and squashing it right then and there, instead of letting it get swept under the rug.

Amanda: Communication is key! You're not always going to be in that honeymoon phase. You have to keep it real, but all in love. It took us a long time to really grasp this. If we would let it build, it'll just blow up in our faces. We had to try and understand the other even if we did not agree with each other. We would respect each other's feelings and try to find a solution to the issue.

Bryan: Another admirable trait is that you guys are very convicted when it comes to your relationship with God, and you don't let society dictate your beliefs. That can be a real challenge for people your age because there is sort of an "anything goes" attitude now. Have you had to remove relationships with people over your walk with God and what it means to you?

Nate: We never had to really remove relationships. We have a very close circle of friends, which is mainly our family. There was never a time that we had to stop talking to people.

Amanda: I think the people in my life who don't share the same views, we respect each other enough to not let it affect the relationship.

Bryan: Was it difficult to leave your old church and come to Liquid, and do you feel a different connection with friends from church?

Nate: Yes. Our old church was mainly family, so it was hard to leave. It was hard at first due to the size of Liquid, but we knew that this would be our new home. We started meeting people, getting to know people, and started to develop a true relationship with some people. It's easier to maintain the relationships now because we both genuinely trust each other.

Amanda: It's much easier to relate to someone that I know through church. It also means I have people I can call and ask them to pray over me if I'm going through something hard. A church friend would understand my faith without me having to explain it.

Bryan: You guys are expecting a son in October, and I know that God and Christianity will be central in raising him. How excited, scared, nervous, elated, etc. are you both at impending parenthood?

Nate: I am beyond excited to meet him, but also nervous in raising him, if that makes sense. I am worried that I will fail him in some way, and I don't ever want that day to happen. But I know that comes with every parent and child relationship. I'm super-excited to just hold him, kiss him, and raise him for the rest of our lives. It's going to be a blast.

Amanda: I feel every single emotion in the book. I always knew a relationship with God was important. But now bringing a child into this dark world, I know now more than ever I want my son to know God's love. Not by forcing the Bible or church on him, but by simply living every day for God and letting him see that from such a young age.

Bryan: Nate, how impactful has music been on your walk with God?

Nate: Beyond impactful. That is the main reason why I consider myself so close to Him is because of music. I was raised on the worship team, playing piano, bass, drums, singing. My dad always wanted me involved in some sort of way, so it was always a thing in my life. Worship was always there. Whenever I felt depressed, worship was there. It's all I knew my whole life, and that will never change.

Bryan: Amanda, if you could tell your younger self one thing when it came to Christianity, what would it be?

Amanda: I would tell my younger self you have no idea how loved and seen you are. Even in the darkest period of your life, there is a light with an overwhelming love looking down on you. You will get through the storm, and you will face different challenges in life. But depression will never hold you. Anxiety will never define you. You have a God who died because he loves you so much and so that you may live. Name a better, truer love than that. Just hold on mama, it'll get better.

Bryan: Finally, being an example of a good Christian can sometimes be challenging today. What is your biggest takeaway on what it means to be a Christian?

Nate: Honestly, to be yourself. Some people think that because they are Christian that they have to act all holy. You can be a cool Christian [*laughs*]. Being a Christian of course has its ups and downs, and you go through so many seasons. But you have to remember the person that is watching from above guiding you through it all. He knows everything, knows everything that is and will happen to you. It's all in His plan for more good things to come. Being a Christian is hard, but it's also amazing, and I don't think I would ever leave God's hand again.

Amanda: Don't lose faith. We live in a world where even as a Christian, darkness can easily consume you. But one thing I do know is the light in the dark is so much brighter. Find that light breaking through when you are going through a tough season and don't let go. Let it drive you, let that small light be your faith. Take it day by day. This walk is not easy and that's okay. But it's so worth it!

Nate currently serves as the Worship Leader at Liquid Church's broadcast campus, is the graphic designer at Insignia, which is the parent company of Tribl, Maverick City Music and Housefires and has his own design company, https://edencrtv.com/. The couple are the owners of edencltv, edencltv.com, a clothing brand that is about to launch. Amanda works in the HR field and the couple are awaiting the arrival of their son, Noah, this October.

Kyle and Michell Ellsworth

Bryan: What were your spiritual lives like growing up?

Michell: I grew up Catholic. It was interesting because my family was very religious in a sense, but also, not really. It was more like those Catholics that would go to church on Sundays or the big holidays, but then would be so self-righteous in the world. But I grew up also going to a church where what you were mattered more than what you do.

So, they really cared much more about your making sure that you were a good Catholic in presence, but it didn't really matter what was in your heart or what you were doing once you were outside of the church. That was very weird to me.

I feel like I always have questions now because of the way I grew up. It was like you had to earn your way into Heaven and there was also so much about going to hell. "You're gay, you're going to hell. You talk back to your parents, you're not going to Heaven." That made me push religion to the side, because what I was being told did not hold true to my values. I still believed in God, but I kind of didn't want to be part of that scene.

Bryan: How old were you when you started withdrawing?

Michell: Around eight, but I couldn't fully do it, because my stepdad wouldn't allow me to make my own decisions. It was his way or the highway.

Bryan: Were you here in America when this happened, or were you still in Colombia?

Michell: No, I was here. I think when I came to the United States, my stepdad was even more strong in faith than anybody that I was raised with. He would literally make us kneel every Friday for like an hour while he recited the Resurrection from start to finish. If I got tired and started sitting, oh, all hell would break loose, literally.

Then, I started asking questions like, "Where in the Bible does it say this?" Or "What about this?" That was, to him, like, "How dare you, you atheist? How are you questioning God?" So, I think all that just came into fruition, and I was like, "I don't think that I really believe all that you believe." I think I slowly started pulling away, and then he stopped doing it. He stopped making us sit as long, because he started really focusing on his work, and stopped being as present and as around. So, we just stopped doing things altogether. We stopped going to church. We still believed, and we still prayed, but not in the same way.

Bryan: What about you, Kyle?

Kyle: I grew up baptized into the Lutheran religion, and it was only my biological father that would take my sister and I to church. My parents got divorced when I was three. My mom was part of the Catholic religion but was okay with me being under the Christian religion with my father. Because of the divorce I saw my dad every other weekend. That lasted until I was nine.

I started moving away going into my pre-teenage years not believing in religion or having a father figure or a mother figure that would take us to church. I never got active into church until like six years ago.

Bryan: It does not seem like either of you completely disconnected from your belief in God, though.

Michell: I think I've always been very strong in my faith regarding believing in God. It turned into me picking and choosing what the Lord calls us to do or not to do. Even though we stopped going to church, God was always at the center of our lives. I don't think I ever completely lost and disconnected myself from God. Religion, yes, but not God.

Bryan: Did you see religion as more of rules and regulations rather than being cared for?

Michell: Religion was like the law when I was growing up. Religion to me was doing things to make yourself look like a good person, like going to church, but you did not put into practice what was taught. Religion to me was like putting on an act when I was growing up.

Kyle: For me, just the trials and tribulations that I went through were kind of what separated me from the church. Probably the one thing my biological father did right in my life was trying to get us to go to church and to be a part of a church community. I am sure he's still a God-fearing man.

In high school I became a typical teenager. I did not have time for church. I would stay up late on Saturdays, then sleep in all day Sunday. So, church was never a thing for me.

Bryan: Was that more because you weren't being brought to church at that point or because you didn't care anymore?

Kyle: I think it was because I did not have any religious figures in my life. None of my friends went to church. None of them were religious. They didn't talk about it. It was never a conversation that was brought up. I was still living with my mom, and she didn't go to church or anything like that.

Now, Michell and I hunger for ways that we can relate to God and how that works in our lives, in the present. But as a child, only having that minimal exposure, I never had the curiosity to find out more growing up.

Michell: When we first started dating, I was still living my life believing in God, but picking and choosing what I followed. Living with a significant other, what's wrong with that? In my head, it was "Yes, live with the significant other so you know if you can handle this person for the rest of your life." I am a very practical person, so everything is rooted in practicality. When we first started dating, we were having sexual relations. We were living together. We weren't practicing any things that the Lord calls us to when in a God-centered relationship.

Bryan: When did that shift to where you are start?

238

Michell: Before we started dating, Kyle was coming to Liquid Church already, and he was heavily involved in Liquid Family. Then, we started dating, and you stopped going as much, I think.

Kyle: Work started getting in the way because of my Sunday schedule. I was transferred from one store to another store, which is where we met.

Michell: We went to Rhode Island one year right before the holidays, and we went to Sunday service at his sister's church. I remember yearning for a church community like hers. It was totally different than what I grew up with. Nobody cared if you wore Sunday best, or that your kid was crying or not. Everybody cared that your heart was in the right place, and that you were there to be loved fully for who you were. That was something I really wanted in our lives.

I told Kyle that I wanted to go back to Liquid, and we made a New Year's resolution, and went to the first service of that year.

Kyle: That was the start of God lining things up in our lives.

Michell: From that point on, we never stopped going. When we went back, we got heavily into serving. He dove in on the media team. He literally followed Rick [Mostacero] around and was like, "Excuse me. You. I want to do what you're doing."

When we started serving together, I fell more in love with him watching him serve others. We also started spending time praying together as well and that also strengthened our relationship.

Kyle: Serving was turning me into the man God wanted me to be.

Bryan: With that deep dive in, you decided to live separately and Michell, you moved back home. Was that hard for you guys to live apart again during your engagement?

Kyle: For me it became something to look forward to once we were married. It was more exciting to live that year apart. She said she wanted to get married a year to the day that we got engaged. So, we had two things to look forward to. The wedding and moving back in together.

Michell: I got used to not living with him again during that year, so it did become something to look forward to. I feel like God has a specific way of doing things. After moving back home, my mom and sister saw me going through this faith journey and I think that had an impact on him. I felt like it made our connection stronger. I was able to support my mom more. She and I always had more of a sister relationship than a mother-daughter one. She had me when she was 21, so it has always been that way. I ended up being happy we set that goal to move back in together because it also gave me a chance to mourn having to move out again and not being with my mom and sister.

Kyle: It also led to me being asked by a leader to chat with one of our members who was going through a similar challenge of living together before marriage. It is cool the way God works in that His teachings were not just used for us, but we passed those along to another couple.

Michell: I wanted our house to have a firm foundation in God, so living apart and abstaining from sex became something to be proud of. It also cemented in my mind that Kyle is the person I wanted to marry. When he asked me to marry him, it was an immediate yes and I was so excited. But then I started asking myself if I could be with him the rest of my life? I had a conversation with God, and He spoke to me, assuring me we had a firm foundation.

We also went through marriage mentoring at church, which we took very seriously. It strengthened our skill of talking things through. We started doing devotionals as a couple. In the marriage mentoring we did a lot of devotionals and conflict resolution talking. We both have different love languages and the way he hears things is not the way I hear things. We had to work through that.

240

I have had the privilege of watching Kyle transition from a manager of a store to working at Liquid. He did not really connect with people when he worked in retail. He was always friendly with co-workers, but also put walls up. He has always been a people person. People would always gravitate toward him, but he would not let them completely in. When I see him leading now, I see how much he genuinely loves the people he serves with, but is also open and vulnerable with people.

Bryan: When you started really digging into your walk with God, did you lose friendships because of the change?

Kyle: I think we had already found those friends who encouraged us and wanted us to be followers of Christ.

Michell: It also happened very fast for us. When we went back to church that January, we ended up getting baptized down the Jersey Shore in May. I was also in a small group by then at church with other Christian sisters.

Kyle: I was also in a small group who supported us.

Michell: We are very fortunate to have people in our lives at church that have been married a little longer and we learn different things from them, and they have been very open with sharing their wisdom with us and praying for us. I think it is important to have people you can lean on, outside of your husband or wife, because you can't expect them to take on everything you are going through. You need people on the outside, and we are very lucky that we have people guiding us to the Lord.

Kyle is the Facilities Director at Liquid Church's main campus in Parsippany. Michell is the Student Assistance Counselor and the Anti-Bullying Specialist at West Morris Central High School. She also is a mental health therapist at Center For Assessment and Treatment. The couple recently celebrated their first wedding anniversary.

Victor Cardona

Bryan: What was your spiritual life like growing up?

Victor: I grew up in a Pentecostal home, and my mom and dad had our family in church seven days a week! Sunday there were two services, Monday we had Bible study, Tuesday we had Christian boys club, Wednesday we had Bible study, Thursday we had some church event, Friday was youth night, and Saturday there was always some conference to go to.

Thankfully, I was friends with most of the teens at church, which made the experience fun and *not* overwhelming. Although annoying as a teen at times, I thank God because it kept me out of trouble. Who knows where I would be if it were not for my parents? I thank God every day for good parenting.

Bryan: Did you drift from your spirituality when you were in high school, college and your younger adult years?

Victor: I drifted away many times over the years. All throughout school the temptation was always there, but my parents also always had us involved with the local church. I remember missing many school events, sports, and friends' parties because of church events. I hated it and wished I didn't, but I guess there was a silver lining to it all! God kept me safe throughout the years.

Before my current wife and through a failed relationship in my early 20s, I drifted away for a few years to find myself. I was heavy into the club scene with daily alcohol consumption. After the split was the most difficult. I was young, inexperienced, and not happy with the way I physically looked. I remember a few breakdowns at my home and on the beach where I literally cried to God. After I finally let out what I was holding in, I began to heal.

After the last breakdown, I started drafting a plan to return to the feet of Christ, get into tip-top physical shape, build mental stability, and reignite my passion for life. Although the times I drifted away were difficult, I thank God for them, as they made me who I am today. I have grown and learned from them because of the consequences.

Bryan: When did you decide to fully submit yourself to God and his calling for your life and what do you feel that calling is?

Victor: Although I always feel like there is room for improvement, I fully committed to God in my mid-20s as I was learning to navigate life and become a man.

I'm pretty sure I figured out my calling during Covid when everyone was having a mental breakdown. I had an epiphany on the word love. There wasn't a lot of loving going on through the pandemic with social media, media outlets injecting fear, the political/social divide, etc.

I feel as if my calling is literally to love on people. Always extend love first, then ask questions second. Extend a smile, give someone a hug, make them laugh, listen to what's going on, be intentional with looking into their eyes, and encourage everyone around you. Make the room a better place when you walk in. I love people. I look at the best in everyone. My No. 1 calling is to extend God's love and hope to everyone, *not* just Christians or people in my demographic.

Bryan: You have a beautiful family, which in and of itself is a gift from Him. How do you lead as a father and husband?

Victor: It isn't an easy task and I'm surely not perfect. It's a daily "Come to Jesus" meeting every morning between God and me. I pray for strength, wisdom, peace, healing, and God's grace over my family every day. I always try to act in love and patience, although it can be tough with a two-year-old and four-year-old.

When we are not traveling as a family, we try to be as involved as possible in our local church and ensure that we are speaking about the teachings of Jesus through all situations.

As a father, I am intentional about spending quality time with them, even if it's for 30 minutes during the week. When I am with them, I am not on social media or my laptop. I tell them I love them three to four times a day. I usually book a short family weekend trip once a month so we can spend quality time together as a family as we all live busy lives.

As a husband, I wish I could say I was a better leader. My wife is the saint and the rock of my family. She keeps us going and is the queen of our home. Where I am given the opportunity, I lead by example. I encourage her through tough situations, always love her and check on her, and try to listen in when times are rough. I'm not perfect, but I am getting better. We hired a nanny to come watch the kids once a week so I can date my wife all over again. We also try to get away as a couple with no kids twice a year.

Bryan: You are also very successful in business and are always hanging out with other guys. How important have they been on your walk with God?

Victor: Success can mean different things to different people. I define my success by the joy and peace that my family has. I am naturally an extrovert and enjoy being in the presence of others. That includes friends and family. Of my closest friends, there are a few who stand out as those who have been instrumental in my walk with Christ. They will tell me like it is and won't be bashful on relaying the message that I am slacking as a spiritual leader to my family. One of my best friends drove an hour in 2017 to tell me that "I fell off and needed to get my life back in order with Christ!" Talk about a wakeup call.

Bryan: What are some of the activities that you do with them or your family that are Christ-centered?

Victor: I should honestly do more. My wife prays with our kids every evening. When we are not traveling, we are faithful to our local church and enjoy life groups, volunteer opportunities, and other fellowship nights. We always look for opportunities and conversations to relate situations to the Bible or characters from the Bible.

Bryan: Who has been one of your biggest mentors on your walk with God?

Victor: First and foremost, mentors in all areas are crucial to your progress. Mentors or coaches in your walk with God, business coaching, personal fitness, etc.

There are a few that come to mind. I have a few friends that are business leaders and executives, these men are also men of God, and they have beautiful families. We talk about all things, including faith, parenting, spirituality, business, family, etc. I try to get with one of the executives monthly for coffee just to talk about life. I always seek his advice for prayer on any big decisions. I recently remember an instance where I asked him how I should deal with a situation with my kids at school. It's the little things that make a big difference.

Bryan: Has there ever been a time in your life where you have asked God "why"?

Victor: As funny as it sounds, I don't ask God why. I usually know why or understand that most of the circumstances I am in are because of my own choices. If it is something that is completely out of my control, I'm optimistic and believe that all things will work out according to His will. The faith muscle isn't an easy muscle to build, but it's getting stronger and stronger. I believe that everything in life happens for you and not to you. Instead of asking "why," you should ask "What can I learn from this?"

Bryan: How did He respond to you and what did you do to enact change?

Victor: I can say that every response is usually a consequence. There is a consequence for good behavior and not so good behavior. Those consequences usually present themselves in my body, family, health, mindset, etc. Once I see one of those areas take a hit, I pivot and push for change immediately. It is not easy, but it is necessary for growth.

Bryan: Raising children today is a challenge with the issues facing youth. In what ways have you (and will you) chat with your kids about issues?

Victor: I haven't reached the age where my kids are facing these issues as the little ones are two and four years old. It's not as simple or black and white as parents think.

With that said, I believe in complete and total transparency with your kids. No topic is off the table and should be discussed with an open mind, love, and understanding. In all things and in every way, speak and blanket all conversations with love. I also believe that church and schooling and education starts and ends at home. In the same way you don't expect your kids to only hear the word of God on Sundays, you shouldn't expect the same for the education and social system. Our home is their fortress, and we will tackle all issues head-on with love and openness. Church, school, gangs, social media, and TV are not meant to raise my kids. Parents raise their kids with God's help!

Bryan: If people were to see photos of you, your family, hanging out with friends, business get-togethers, they would assume you have the perfect life. In what areas do you still struggle and ask God for help?

Victor: That's funny. Come see photos of us around 8 p.m. when it's time to put the kids to sleep! Let's also trade places when the girls are up at 6 a.m. screaming and whining for snacks or ice cream!

In all seriousness, I'm the least perfect man in existence. I'm a broken man saved by grace and someone who fails daily. I have made more mistakes than the average person. I still struggle with bad thoughts and insecurities as an executive, father, and husband every day. Things are usually not rosy.

I have heavily relied on God's grace, His word, and controlling my thoughts through prayer and meditation. I adopted the principle of early rising a few years back to get back into shape. Waking up between 4 a.m. to 5 a.m., praying/meditation, reading, writing, exercising, etc. In addition to my early rituals, I try to stay active at the gym and other activities at my local club.

Bryan: Do you have routines and rituals with your own kids, so they keep their interest in God going?

Victor: My family can always do better, but we pray every evening and look to inject Christ in every situation or discussion. When we are not traveling, and are involved at our local church at all events, volunteer opportunities, etc.

Bryan: What Bible verse stands out for you to lean on for strength?

Victor: Philippians 4:13. All day, every day. The literal word used is I can do *all* things through Christ. Not some, but *all* things.

Victor is a consultant with Enterprise Cybersecurity. He and his wife, Anyis, have two daughters, Skylar and Harlow.

James Apap

Bryan: Tell me about your earliest experiences with spirituality growing up.

James: Spirituality has always been a part of my life for as far back as I can remember. More specifically, a relationship with Jesus. For the most part, I feel that my parents (mainly my mom), did a great job not forcing us to believe. We were made aware of the blessing and faithfulness of God at every pivotal moment.

I remember growing up and never realizing that we didn't have money. We were pretty poor. My dad lost his job, and my mom was working for a Christian school because she wanted us to have a Christian education. My mom told us stories of times where groceries were just dropped off on our front porch. Christmastime must have always been tough financially, but my parents always gave us a great time. They always reminded us of His faithfulness when He provided.

Bryan: Did you ever distance yourself from the church in your teen/young adult years?

James: There was a period, in my late teens or early 20s, when something happened with my brother, and he was arrested. We didn't really get the support we needed from the church. I will admit that it didn't really rattle my faith in God as much as it rattled my faith in my church. I didn't feel cared for by the people who I was in church with for most of my life. That hurt. I stopped serving around that time and started partying a lot more.

Bryan: At what point in your life did you decide to turn it over to God and follow his calling for you?

James: I hit a point where I had to attend to the things I thought would make me happy. Wife, kids, and a house with a white fence. They did not. I was doing something I love and making six figures doing it. I realized I still felt like it wasn't enough and so I started seeking God for answers.

He placed on my heart to quit the gym, where I had been working for 12-plus years. This was extremely difficult because at the time I was making more money than my wife was. He led me to inquire about working for my church.

Bryan: Many people have looked to you as a mentor, me included, which you take very seriously. How long did it take you to feel confident in being one?

James: I always liked being able to listen to people and give them advice and perspective. I tend to use a lot of personal experience and analogies to lead and mentor people. This helps people see and understand what I am saying better. They also know I am coming from a place of personal experience.

Bryan: Who were/are some of your mentors?

James: At the moment I don't really have one. When I was younger, I had a great mentor who really helped ignite a passion for student ministry.

Bryan: You also have mentored high school and college students. What speaks to you about mentoring them specifically?

James: Those years are some of the most important times in their lives, but we tend to put some pressure on them both as parents and the students do it to themselves. I just listen and be there if ever they reach out. I also have seen that the students I have mentored usually are the ones helping to lead and mentor my kids.

Bryan: You have had quite a journey, both professionally and personally. Talk a little about the challenges that were presented to you.

James: I can't say that I get this right all the time. Especially in difficult times. I have gone through a tough period in my marriage, and I thought I was going to get divorced from my wife. I turned to God and allowed Him to breathe life back into my marriage.

With Liquid it has been an interesting journey. Being recently let go from working there really threw me for a loop. No one prepares you for the emotional rollercoaster after being let go from your church job. God has been faithful throughout this process (that I am still in the middle of). He has given me an amazingly supportive wife. I must admit that I know God has something for me, but I am a little impatient with Him and want an answer right now.

Bryan: You have been at a crossroads recently. How have you been able to lean into the word and prayer for help in navigating that?

James: In the middle of this crossroad, it has been difficult. I am looking for direction from God and (not patiently) waiting on Him. I do this by actively looking for Him to speak to me through His word, through messages I am listening to, and through my family and friends. You get knocked around when trying to navigate uncharted waters, but I know that He is with me and won't let me go!

Bryan: Is there a specific book of the Bible or verse that gets you through the tough moments?

James: Jeremiah 29:11 is one of my favorites. I always turn back to this one. "For I know the plans I have for you," says the Lord. "They are plans for good and not for disaster, to give you a future and a hope. In those days when you pray, I will listen."

James has served in various roles in youth ministry and with at-risk youth. He and his wife, Cintya, share two sons, Mateo and Josiah.

Acknowledgements

First and foremost, I have to thank God. Without His presence in my life, I would not be where I am today.

To everyone who participated, it means so much that you were willing to share your walk with God in the book. You have all inspired me in multiple ways.

To my mother, Nancy, and my sister, Jill, you are the two strongest women I know. I do not know how you put one foot in front of the other after all we have been through. It's only by the grace of God that we are all here and stay close.

My nephews, Danny and Cameron, I love you guys more than anything in the world. You are growing into incredible young men and I am so proud of you.

My brother-in-law, Danny, thank you for being the rock when we were all crumbling at a time you needed to crumble, too. All of us, my mom, myself, sister, and the boys, have depended on your strength.

Mr. & Mrs. "Mama" Gleeson, you are always interested in what I am up to and have provided such love and support over the years.

Clint Taylor, Rick Mostacero, Cuyler Black and Tee Fields, thank you for being mentors to me. It is not always easy, but I am so glad that God put you four in my life. I honestly would not be where I am at this point on my walk with God without you.

Abby Taylor, there are not enough adjectives to describe just how beautiful of a human being you are. You are the kindest, most genuine, loving person I know.

Kyle Ellsworth, Rich Lem and David Ramirez, thank you for taking me under your wing and allowing me to grow in God's timing.

To the lead team at Liquid Church – Dave Brooks, Pastor Tim Lucas, Pastor Kayra Montañez and Hyo Sil Siegel, thank you for having faith in me, seeing who God called me to be and allowing me to flourish as a volunteer staff member at Liquid Church.

Vicky Chan, your kindness and faith in me means so much.

Michell Ellsworth, Sharon Chiang and Katherine Hernandez, thank you for walking alongside me and for the support you gave as I grew closer to God.

Tommy Do, Phil Gallo and James Apap, my brothers from another mother, thank you for lifting me up, encouraging me and equally as important, the laughter.

Robyn Philpotts, thank you for always being there for me.

Pastor Mike Lee, it is such a pleasure to serve alongside you, and you have become an important source of support and guidance in my life.

Deby Fabrazzo, Julissa Rodriguez and Gary Casaletto, thank you for all of the time you have spent with me as I navigated trying to reconcile my past and my present.

To the entire staff of Liquid Church, you have all embraced me with open arms, encouraged me, prayed for me, fought for me, supported me, helped me grow and continue to do so. Liquid Church is truly my home away from home.

To the Liquid Worship team, thank you for always making my connection to God a direct line. Your passion and giftings really do bring people closer to Him.

For everyone that has ever supported me and continues to do so, you have my undying gratitude. If I listed each of you, the acknowledgements page would be longer than the book itself.

Nate Goyco, what you did bringing my vision to life on the cover is just phenomenal. If anyone reading the book needs a graphic designer, check him out at https://edencrtv.com/

John Steinheimer, thank you for doing an incredible job on the images that appear on the cover.

Jennifer Wislocki, thank you for all that you did in getting myself and Pastor Justin linked up and the care you took with his interview.

Michael Davis, I appreciate all that you did to coordinate my interview with Josh and for all of the subsequent follow-up afterward.

Finally, to Amy E. Gross, who met a massive deadline and worked tirelessly on the editing to make this book the best it could be, I am incredibly grateful.

Made in the USA
Middletown, DE
15 September 2022

10475155R00151